The Empire's Smallest Regiment

The Gambia Company of the West African Frontier Force, 1902-1958

The Empire's Smallest Regiment

The Gambia Company of the West African Frontier Force, 1902-1958

Charles J. Estep

To
Mom, Dad, and Gabby

Library and Archives Canada Cataloguing in Publication
Estep, Charles, author
The Empire's Smallest Regiment / Charles Estep

Issued in print and electronic formats.
ISBN: 978-1-990644-13-9 (soft cover)
ISBN: 978-1-990644-14-6 (e-book)

Editor: Phil Halton
Cover design: Leif Perry

Double Dagger Books Inc.
Toronto, Ontario, Canada
www.doubledagger.ca

ACKNOWLEDGEMENTS

The Empire's Smallest Regiment is based on the Master's thesis I completed at the University of Calgary in the fall of 2020 under the expert guidance of Dr. Tim Stapleton. I am grateful and very much appreciative of the support and guidance that Dr. Stapleton provided throughout the entire research and writing process. Additionally, Dr. David Bercuson and Dr. Rowland "Caesar" Apentiik were invaluable for their insights and opinions as part of my defense committee.

I would also like to thank my professors, and now colleagues, at the United States Air Force Academy who helped foster my passion for History. Dr. Mark Grotelueshen and Dr. "Doc" Bob Wettemann showed me the value in understanding, applying, and sharing important history, especially within the context of the profession of arms.

Lastly, this book would not have been possible without the support and dedication of the Double Dagger team. Phil Halton was instrumental in the editing process and helped ensure that the Gambia Company's story can be shared with a much wider audience across the world.

Table of Contents

A Note on Terminology

It is necessary to explain the nomenclature and terminology used in this discussion. In many instances, I use the colonial names given to places and organizations. For example, the current Gambian city of Banjul is referred throughout by its colonial name of Bathurst. This is done for simplification and continuity throughout the entire work. When necessary, the modern, postcolonial equivalent of the colonial terminology is given in parentheticals.

Bathurst – Banjul
British East Africa – Kenya
British Somaliland – Republic of Somaliland
Burma – Myanmar
Creole – Krio
Fernando Po – Bioko
German East Africa – Burundi, Rwanda, and Mainland Tanzania
German South West Africa – Namibia
Gold Coast – Ghana
James Island – Kunta Kinteh Island
Northern Rhodesia – Zambia
Rangoon – Yangon
Spanish Muni – Equatorial Guinea
Tanganyika – Tanzania
Togoland – Togo and parts of Ghana

Abbreviations

BTU – Bathurst Trade Union
CAR – Central African Regiment
CSM – Company Sergeant Major
FEA – French Equatorial Africa
FWA – French West Africa
GCR – Gold Coast Regiment
GOC – General Officer Commanding
GR – Gambia Regiment
IEF – Indian Expeditionary Force
IG – Inspector General
KAR – King's African Rifles
LMG – Light Machine Gun
MLB – Military Labour Bureau
NCO – Noncommissioned Officer
NR – Nigeria Regiment
OC – Officer Commanding
RAC – Royal African Corps
RSM – Regimental Sergeant Major
RWAFF – Royal West African Frontier Force (WAFF received the royal designation in 1928)
SEAC – Southeast Asia Command
SLB – Sierra Leone Battalion
SLR – Sierra Leone Regiment
VD – Venereal Disease
WA – West African
WAC – West Africa Command
WAFF – West African Frontier Force
WAR – West African Regiment
WIR – West India Regiments

Introduction

THE BRITISH REGIMENTAL SYSTEM sought to establish a distinct martial culture and *espirit de corps* among soldiers. After 1881 and what historian David French terms the Cardwell-Childers Reforms, the British revamped the regimental system to foster unique regimental identities and provide military organizations with enough competency to achieve successes in a global empire.Through symbols, traditions, and customs, the British sought to manufacture military culture and identity within regiments. French argues that "Regiments were culturally defined organizations that were bound together by shared historical memories, customs, and a myth of descent, not by the common ethnic or local origins of its members...The idea of 'the regiment' was something that was artificially constructed."[1] In effect, the regiment became an "imagined community."[2]

Similar to their British counterparts, African soldiers serving in British-led colonial militaries were placed within the regimental system that promoted manufactured martial identities and inclusion in an imagined military community. African soldiers were organized into local regiments, which fostered and celebrated unique regimental identities. However, not every African colonial military organization was given the privilege to establish a regimental identity and celebrate its past accomplishments. Throughout the majority of its history, the Gambia Company of the West African Frontier Force (WAFF) was barred from such a right, even though it possessed many of the features of a regiment and routinely evidenced its military value in combat. A regiment maintains its own identity, culture, and institutional independence relative to other military organizations. The Gambia Company expressed these requirements, but regimental status was denied until the Second World War. In fact, officers seconded to the Gambia Company even noted the company's regimental qualities.[3] British officials pointed to the Gambia Company's small size, below battalion strength, as grounds against granting regimental status; ordinarily, British regiments were the size of two battalions. However, it was also the Gambia's perceived insignificance within the greater British Empire that delayed the Gambia Company from gaining official recognition of its storied military reputation. The Gambia, a small sliver of land completely surrounded by French territory, was largely unwanted by British colonial officials and routinely offered to France for territorial exchange. Some British officers and colonial officials serving in the Gambia wished to gain regimental status for the Gambia Company, but British officials in London did not want to foster a regimental identity based on respected British military traditions in an undesired territory. Eventually, after almost fifty years of being in existence, the Gambia Company finally received regimental distinction, making it one of the smallest regiments within the British Empire.

This book does not offer a comprehensive history of the Gambia, nor does it represent a complete history of the British colonial military in West Africa. Rather, I attempt to provide the first academic study of the colonial military history of the Gambia during the first half of the twentieth century, a topic on which the greater historiography of Britain's African colonial military has largely been silent.

Section One discusses the early years of the Gambia Company. I argue that policies concerning the company's formation initially limited its development into an efficient, independent military organization. The Gambia Company formed from a nucleus of Sierra Leoneans, and continued to rely on Sierra Leonean recruits. British officials actively limited the company's development into an all-Gambian force out of fears of Gambian disloyalty and continued belief in eventual administrative takeover by the French.

Section Two discusses the Gambia Company during the First World War. I argue that despite its smallness and independence, the Gambia Company played a valuable role in the Cameroon and East Africa campaigns of the war. Through its active involvement in the African campaigns, the Gambia Company developed into an effective and respected military organization.

Section Three discusses the Gambia Company during the interwar period. I argue that during this period the company finally transitioned into an all-Gambian force and secured its institutional independence following British realization that the Gambia would remain a British territory. However, imperial strategic concerns and training deficiencies eventually forced the Gambia Company's attachment to the Sierra Leone Battalion.

Section Four discusses the greatly expanded Gambia Company during the Second World War. I argue that through military expansion in West Africa, the Gambia contributed disproportionately to imperial defense compared to the rest of British West Africa. Additionally, the discussion shows that the now renamed Gambia Regiment contributed significantly to the Allied war effort fighting in the Burma campaign. Ultimately, this micro-historical analysis of the Gambia Company aims to expose the greater trends, dynamics, and features of the British colonial military in West Africa.

This work is important because it exposes the previously ignored history of the only colonial military unit in the Gambia who kept Gambian soldiers within its ranks. Of course, *The Empire's Smallest Regiment* will be valuable for any reader interested in Gambian history and the military history of greater West Africa. However, the book is useful for any student interested in the military and racial dynamics that accompanied British attempts to establish, maintain, and protect their global empire, especially within Africa. I hope to carry on the work of past African military historians to highlight the experiences of ordinary Gambian soldiers through a historical analysis of the Gambia Company. Previous operational and regimental histories mention the company in passing, but never explore its actions within various conflicts in depth.

During my research, I examined documents from both the National Archives of the United Kingdom located at Kew and the Gambia National Archives in Banjul, while also referencing numerous official accounts of operations written by British military officers. These sources are valuable in uncovering the top-down history of the colonial military in the Gambia, but there are some limitations. Written by either British colonial officials or military officers, the documents often promote the British point of view and fail to accurately represent the African voice. Within the colonial context, British mindsets were often corrupted by racist and other beliefs, which translated into one sided and paternalistic accounts of military related events.

Furthermore, the content of these documents is important. Many of the documents relating specifically to the Gambia Company were annual reports, compiled by the British inspector general of the WAFF, that discussed training, recruiting, organization, and establishment. In other words, these documents did not capture the entire experience of ordinary Gambian soldiers within the Gambia Company.

I also cite memoirs of British officers who served with the Gambia Company which are located at the Weston Library in Oxford, England as part of the Oxford Records Development Project, compiled around 1980. These memoirs provide greater clarity on day-to-day operations and interactions between British officers and African soldiers within the Gambia Company; but similar to the official government and military documents, they promote the British point of view through paternalistic accounts. Additionally, these memoirs only relate to the Second World War era, as other periods concerning the Gambia Company are not covered. The biggest problem associated with all of these sources is that they lack the African perspective.

A few African soldiers who served elsewhere with the WAFF did write down their experiences in memoirs or participate in interviews, but this largely did not occur in the Gambia.[4] Rather, in order to relate a more thorough history of the colonial military in the Gambia, I utilize previously ignored documents, such as award citations, and highlight fragments of colonial documents that give insight into the experience of Gambian soldiers. Additionally, the discussion places the Gambian soldier, and the greater Gambia Company, within the context of larger events. Stories of the service of ordinary Gambian soldiers are largely lost to history, but I seek to expose the Gambian perspective through what sources are available. Unfortunately, the nature of the historical evidence limits a complete bottom-up view of the colonial military in the Gambia. Despite these limitations, I hope to convey the valuable and important history of the colonial military in the Gambia.

Section One

The Origins and Formation of the Gambia Company

EUROPEAN POWERS HAD SUBSTANTIAL CONTACT with Sub-Saharan Africa since the 1400s, but it was not until the late nineteenth century "Scramble for Africa" that European colonialism became firmly established on the continent. With the implementation of colonial rule, European powers sought to solidify their authority through the use of military force. They created colonial militaries composed of African soldiers, but led by European officers, in the context of racial hierarchy, to secure authority against local and European competition. Within West Africa, the British established the West African Frontier Force throughout their four West African colonies – the Gambia, Sierra Leone, the Gold Coast (today's Ghana), and Nigeria – to subjugate the local populations under British colonial rule and combat French encroachment on British territory.[1]

In order to explain the formation of the only WAFF unit in the Gambia and the political environment in which it initially served, we must first discuss the development and implementation of British colonialism in the country. The discussion shows that the Gambia Company was a separate entity within the WAFF, constrained by structures and policies that initially limited its development as an independent military organization.

Furthermore, it is necessary to explore the structural and social trends that influenced how the greater WAFF functioned. Analyzing the British colonial military in West Africa through the lens of one infantry company exposes in stark detail the biases and mindsets that informed British officials on forming and administering African colonial militaries.

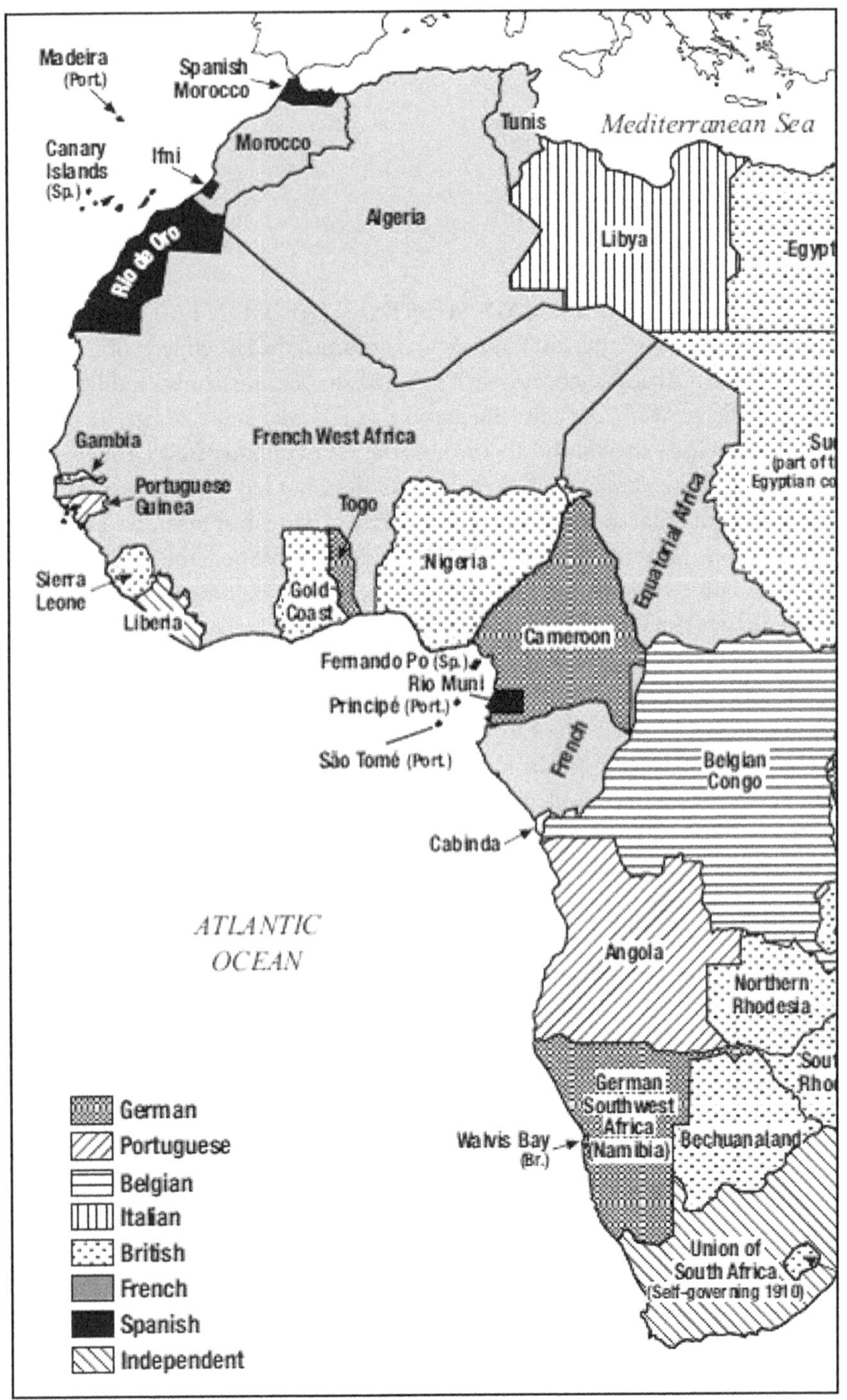
Madeira
(Port.)
Spanish
Morocco
Tunis
Mediterranean Sea
Canary
Islands
(Sp.)
Ifni
Morocco
Algeria
Rio de Oro
Libya
Egypt
Gambia
French West Africa
Portuguese
Guinea
Togo
Sierra
Leone
Liberia
Gold
Coast
Nigeria
Equatorial Africa
Cameroon
Fernando Po (Sp.)
Rio Muni
Principé (Port.)
São Tomé (Port.)
French
Belgian
Congo
Cabinda
ATLANTIC
OCEAN
Angola
Northern
Rhodesia
German
Southwest
Africa
(Namibia)
Walvis Bay
(Br.)
Bechuanaland
Union of
South Africa
(Self-governing 1910)
German
Portuguese
Belgian
Italian
British
French
Spanish
Independent

Chapter 1
Colonial Gambia

THE GAMBIA ROUTINELY CAPTURED THE ATTENTION of European powers seeking lucrative economic opportunities in the pre-colonial and early colonial periods. The first Portuguese explorers reached the River Gambia in 1456, which initiated a robust trading relationship with local peoples. For the rest of the fifteenth century, Portuguese traders established posts along the banks of the River Gambia, with the main commodity traded being enslaved people. However, Portuguese interest in the Gambia largely diminished after the 1480s when Spanish explorers reached the Gold Coast and parts of the Congo and returned with reports of vast amounts of gold and ivory in the newly "discovered" areas. The Gambia was previously believed to be a land of similarly lucrative economic and material opportunities, but as the Portuguese discovered, the river and the surrounding area lacked any substantial reserves of sought-after precious resources. Subsequently, early European interests in Africa shifted elsewhere.[2]

By the mid-sixteenth century, British and French traders began to establish trading relationships and posts within West Africa, with the River Gambia becoming a popular spot for the British. In 1612, the French attempted to establish a colony, which failed miserably due to tropical disease, a recurring problem for early European establishments in the Gambia. Although the emerging European imperial powers were making contacts in the Gambia during this period, substantial efforts to establish sustained trade networks on the River Gambia were lessened by competition from more popular trading centers north at Cape Verde, Goree Island, and the Senegal River. By this time, the Trans-Atlantic Slave Trade had become firmly established along the Atlantic coast of Africa. European merchants traded for enslaved people at various establishments on the coast to supply colonial plantations in the Americas with an exploited labor force. Through this horrid trade, enslaved people became Africa's largest export, as by the nineteenth century a total of 12.8 million Africans would be forcibly removed from their homes and sent across the Atlantic in slave ships.[3] In effect, the demand for slaves from West Africa ensured that the Gambia remained an important area as a valuable source of captives.[4]

As European economic interests were growing in West Africa because of the slave trade, Courland (present day Latvia and parts of Lithuania) sought to use the Gambia as a lucrative location to improve its economic footing relative to other European powers. In 1651, Courlander ships entered the River Gambia and leased James Island (Kunta Kinteh Island) and St. Mary Island from local kings. The Courlanders erected a fort on James Island and trading posts upriver, but with little support from Europe, the establishments failed and fell into the hands of the Dutch West India Company by 1660.[5] This incited growing competition and rivalry between the Dutch and British in the Gambia until the Dutch ultimately receded from the area by the end of the seventeenth century.[6]

By 1677, the French had captured Goree Island from the Dutch, which in effect, made the French and the British the leading European powers in the Senegambia Region, the area encompassing present day Senegal and the Gambia. The French were firmly established in the Cape Verde-Senegal River area, while the British were firmly established on the River Gambia with James Island as a base of operations. Until 1783 and the Treaty of Versailles, which ended the American Revolutionary War, possession of vital trading centers in the Senegambia region shifted between the French and British as a result of conflict in Europe. Important European enclaves in the Gambia – James Island, McCarthy Island, and Albreda – were routinely captured or destroyed by competing powers as a way to undermine their opponent in times of war, while similar tactics were also employed to the north in Senegal. The Treaty of Versailles, however, solidified British control of the River Gambia. It stated that the British had exclusive rights to control trade on the river, but did not give the British territorial control of the area surrounding the river. At the time, territorial conquest and large imperial holdings were not necessarily European intentions in Africa. European presence on the continent was limited by tropical disease and resistance from strong African powers. Consequently, the British were content with control of just the river and its trade.[7]

British interests in the Gambia grew drastically with their efforts to abolish the slave trade. In 1807, the British declared the trade in enslaved people across international waters and in British territories unlawful. With the River Gambia as a British possession, the British sought to strengthen their position on the river to combat the slave trade.[8] In 1816, British Captain Alexander

Grant secured British control over St. Mary Island from the King of Kombo in exchange for British protection of Kombo from local rivals. Previously, St. Mary Island was uninhabited by European traders due to its sandy terrain, but located at the mouth of the River Gambia, the site provided the British with an excellent position to monitor trade on the river.

The British subsequently constructed the town of Bathurst on St. Mary Island, along with a fort to monitor trade. It served as a base for traders and a home for "liberated Africans."

In 1792, the British also established Freetown in Sierra Leone as a settlement for "Black Loyalists" from North America. As British abolition efforts increased after 1807, "liberated Africans" taken from slaving vessels or ports were sent to Freetown and some were subsequently sent elsewhere in West Africa.[9] As a result, "Liberated Africans" constituted a significant proportion of the Freetown and Bathurst populations. "Liberated Africans" sent to Bathurst as indentured workers were referred to as Aku, similar to the Creole (now called Krio) population in Sierra Leone.[10] Bathurst officially became a British colony in 1821, however, it remained under the administrative control of the governor of Sierra Leone until 1888.[11]

Before and during European encroachment into the Gambia, the river was a thriving place for the local population. The river had routinely fallen under the control of West Africa's storied ancient empires, like the Mali (c.1235-c.1670) and Songhai (c.1448-c.1591) Empires, and was an important facilitatorof both trade and transportation in the region. With the Gambia's inclusion in such empires, especially Songhai, Islam slowly spread among its population. Inclusion in the Mali and Songhai Empires allowed local Gambians greater access to Muslim traders and the trans-Sahara trade, as Islam spread throughout the local merchants and lower classes of society, eventually reaching the higher levels of Gambian society by the time of the consolidation of British colonial rule.[12]

Similar to other areas within West Africa, the Gambia is home to a number of different ethnicities with different languages and cultures - the main five being Mandingo (Mandinka), Fula (Fulani), Wolof, Jola, and Serahule. Additionally, due to the Gambia's position relative to Senegal, the area often welcomes a seasonal labor force known as "strange farmers," who come to the Gambia for planting, harvesting, and herding. During the Soninke-Marabout Wars (1850-1890s), the "strange farmers" were hired as mercenary soldiers by both sides.[13]

When the Europeans arrived in the Gambia, they found that the area was not only divided ethnically, but politically as well, with numerous local kingdoms and polities along the river banks. Major kingdoms, like Barra and

Kombo, were well established in the Gambia and their rulers were points of contact with Europeans seeking land or trade influence on the river. These kingdoms usually maintained peaceful relations with Europeans throughout the centuries of contact, as early European conflict in the Gambia was among competing European powers, not with the local population. However, by the 1850s, local disputes and subsequent civil wars within the various kingdoms brought trouble for the Gambia.[14]

The Soninke-Marabout Wars, which began in 1850, ultimately started as a religious conflict. Islam had been practiced by some Gambians for a number of years, but it was not well established among the higher and ruling classes of Gambian society. The Soninkes were local chiefs and other traditional rulers who held power throughout the various Gambian kingdoms. The Marabouts, on the other hand, were teachers and holy men who preached a "purer" form of Islam than what previously existed in the Gambia and were influenced by other Islamist movements in Western Sudan. The Marabouts declared a "holy war" against the Soninkes, as other Muslims in West Africa had done in response to European encroachment and disruptions caused by the Trans-Atlantic Slave Trade since the late eighteenth century.[15] The Marabout's intention was to impose their form of Islam within all of Gambian society and ultimately take over the political structures on the river. By the mid-1870s the Soninkes were largely defeated, but conflict continued in the Gambia. It became increasingly political as Marabout leaders replaced strictly religious objectives with efforts to overthrow rival political leaders and grow their own bases of support. This new phase of the conflict lasted discontinuously for almost 50 years, from 1850 to the 1890s, and its intensity varied from small scale violence between two villages to large scale wars between whole districts involving thousands of combatants.

Although the Soninke-Marabout Wars originated as a local political and religious dispute between Gambians, the British were indirectly involved throughout the duration of the conflict. The Marabouts initially sought British support against the Soninkes, but the British declined as they desired to maintain their favorable relationships with the local rulers. However, British territorial possessions in the Gambia brought them into the conflict with the Marabouts for defensive purposes. On multiple occasions, British led "military expeditions were launched...to mitigate the effects of the wars...rather than to acquire additional territory."[17] In the 1850s, British administrators in the Gambia, including Governors Richard MacDonnell and Luke O'Connor, sought more active participation in the war to remove any threats to British holdings or people in the Gambia; however, the Colonial Office in London emphasized a policy of retrenchment with no unnecessary expenditures and expansion within the Gambia, or the rest of West Africa for that matter. The Colonial Office's cautious policy remained until the onset of the "Scramble for Africa" in 1884, following the Berlin Conference, and increased territorial competition with the French. With their reactionary position to the Soninke-Marabout Wars, the British relied on the Gambia Militia and the West India Regiments (WIR) for protection of European enclaves. As discussed later, the Gambia Militia recruited from the residents of Bathurst, while the WIR was comprised of "liberated African" conscripts and was based in the Caribbean.[18]

With the external slave trade eliminated from the River Gambia by 1816, the British found little value in maintaining a colony there. Bathurst offered an unhealthy environment for Europeans, while the Gambia's administrative subordinance to Sierra Leone ensured that the colony received little to no funds for infrastructure improvement and development. Sierra Leone routinely ran a deficit, which ensured that whatever profits the Gambia did secure often went to the Sierra Leone government and not to development projects in the Gambia. Territories like the Ceded Mile, Albreda, and British Kombo were added to the Gambia Colony by 1840, but such territories were under constant threat from local conflict caused by the Soninke-Marabout Wars.[19] Additionally, the British made only minor advances in the development of trade on the river. The British believed, as did other European powers, that the River Gambia offered access to lucrative resources in the interior. However, numerous British led expeditions past Barrakunda Falls, the natural roadblock that limited European penetration into the interior, proved that such lucrative opportunities largely did not exist.

Enslaved people were no longer traded in the Gambia and British officials now promoted the doctrine of "Legitimate Commerce," which involved the acquisition of raw materials for industrial production in Europe and North America. Although the Trans-Atlantic slave trade was eliminated, domestic slavery persisted among the local population in the Gambia and the rest of West Africa during this period. To fund this commerce, traders and merchants needed to find legal lucrative exports from the Gambia.[20] By the 1850s, groundnut cultivation and trade exploded in the Gambia, which brought some financial successes for the colony. In the past, groundnuts were cultivated in very small quantities in the Gambia, but increasing demand for vegetable oils as a result of the Industrial Revolution prompted a massive increase in groundnut production throughout the Senegambian region. Interestingly, much of the groundnut exports at this time were sent to France and controlled by French traders with the British only receiving duties. As a result, it was perceived by some British officials that France was benefitting the most from the Gambia's lucrative trade rather than the British.[21]

Due to sustained difficulties in the Gambia and the desire to control continuous blocks ofterritory in West Africa, the British entertained offers of territorial exchange with the French. In 1866, the French first offered to exchange settlements on the Ivory Coast, Grand Bassam, and other smaller territories on the West African coast for control of the Gambia, but such proposals initially fell through because "the British government was unable to find any corresponding French territory it actually wanted."[22] By 1870, news of a potential territorial exchange reached the inhabitants of Bathurst, who overwhelmingly opposed the deal and petitioned Parliament to resist any territorial exchange. However, such contention did little to alter British territorial objectives.

The British responded by asking for the territory north of Freetown in Sierra Leone, known as the Mellacourie region (in present-day Republic of Guinea), where France laid claim. Negotiations stalled and were shelved until 1876 when a similar proposal was again sent by the French and ultimately agreed upon by the British. As before, negotiations fell through as the French procrastinated, believing "it would be only a matter of time before the Gambian settlements became French" and they could use the delay to achieve more favorable circumstances.[23]

French delaying tactics in the negotiations coincided with their advance into the interior of West Africa and subsequent territorial conquest. In the 1880s, the early stages of the Scramble for Africa, the French were occupying the interior of West Africa with military forces and signing treaties with local rulers to establish their political authority. The British responded by doing the same in their African spheres of influence. However, the Gambia turned into a unique case of colonial competition between the French and British within West Africa. At the time, the Soninke-Marabout Wars continued to ravage the Gambian hinterland and distracted British colonial officials. During the conflict, the British were busy protecting their small establishments and trade networks, which allowed the French to advance to areas on both banks of the river and begin treaty negotiations with local rulers. The terms as outlined by the Treaty of Versailles (1783) and succeeding documents stated that the British only had control of the River Gambia itself and not the surrounding territory. In effect, the British only maintained authority over territory, like Bathurst, that local rulers ceded to them. Therefore, the French actions to control territory up to the banks of the river were legal, but if completed, essentially made continued British control of the river impossible and unnecessary. The British hastily made territorial treaties with local riverine rulers as a means to combat French encroachment and secure the Gambia as a potential bargaining chip for resumed talks of territorial exchange in West Africa.[24]

In 1889, the French officially recognized British limited territorial authority surrounding the River Gambia; however, territorial boundaries were not established until 1901. Survey parties were appointed by both countries to draw the boundary. In typical colonial fashion, the surveyors agreed on an arbitrary border 10 kilometers from each bank of the River Gambia extending 470 kilometers into the interior from the Atlantic Ocean, with such areas as Kombo remaining under British control. In effect, the Gambia Colony only included the area immediately surrounding Bathurst, while the rest of the territory was split up into protectorates administered by the Gambian colonial government. British officials maintained the belief that the Gambia was "worthless except for bargaining purposes" with the French.[25] In 1904, the French and British resumed talks for a potential territorial exchange, however by the First World War, the French no longer desired an exchange and ceased negotiations outright. The construction of the Dakar-Kayes-Bamako Railway into the interior and the continued development of other ports in French West Africa greatly reduced the Gambia's value to France. Ultimately, the Gambian example attests to the passivity of the British compared to the French in regard to territorial conquest in the Senegambian region during the Scramble for Africa. As a result, the British were "stuck" with a small, arbitrary territory surrounded on three sides by French Senegal.[26] With a total area of approximately 11,000 square kilometers, the Gambia constitutes the smallest country in mainland Africa today.[27]

The period immediately following the final establishment of colonial rule in the Gambia is important for the history of the Gambia Company WAFF due to the belief that the territory would only temporarily remain under British control. The British ultimately secured political control of the Gambia as a means to exchange for territory elsewhere in West Africa; "what was viewed by the delegates who signed the Convention of 1889 as a temporary expedient [however] became a permanent political reality."[28] Thus, the Gambia Company was created from a nucleus of Sierra Leonean recruits under the British mindset that the unit's service in the Gambia would be temporary and limited relative to other WAFF organizations. As we will discuss, this mindset effectively decreased the efficiency of the Gambia Company as an independent military unit in its early years.

Chapter 2
The West India Regiments

UP UNTIL THE SONINKE-MARABOUT WARS, the British military position in the Gambia had been minor and relatively weak. Early forts at James Island or Bathurst were garrisoned by small numbers of troops from the Royal African Corps (RAC), while inhabitants of such settlements, often without any formal military training, formed the Gambia Militia in times of conflict. The RAC was, for the most part, ineffective in the Gambia. Initially its ranks were made up of military convicts from Britain sent to West Africa as a punishment, who often lacked the sense of discipline and duty required within effective military units. Being Europeans, early RAC soldiers routinely succumbed to the harsh environment and diseases of the River Gambia, making service there extremely hazardous and despised. After the Abolition Act of 1807, "liberated Africans" constituted a large proportion of the rank-and-file of the RAC, who were seen as more effective, resistant to disease, and cheaper than white British soldiers. British officers forcibly impressed "liberated Africans," whether taken from slave ships or raided slave forts, for permanent military service throughout West Africa with the RAC. Although freed from slavery, "liberated Africans" were not entirely free in the sense that they served as indentured workers, whether in military or civilian positions, following manumission.[29]

Gradually, British officers came to rely on the conscription of "liberated Africans" as the foundation of Royal African Corps recruiting and British military power in West Africa. This led to what historian Padraic Scanlan termed "militarized abolition," with the British enforcing abolition through extensive military force as a means to increase their military resources, while officers and colonial officials often benefitted financially. In a sense, the RAC, and eventually the West India Regiments, "martialed the labor of former slaves" to military service under the Crown.[30]

In the late eighteenth century, the West India Regiments were formed as a response to the extremely high invalid rate among British soldiers serving in the West Indies. Similar to the conditions in West Africa, the West Indies offered an unhealthy environment rampant with diseases that affected Europeans at disastrous rates.[31] In 1795, Lieutenant General John Vaughan, commander of British forces in the West Indies, argued that the British should form a corps of black soldiers for service in the West Indies based on the observations that they remained healthy and were relatively more resistant to disease within the hazardous tropical environments.[32] The same line of thinking was applied in arguments for the use of black soldiers in West Africa, as seen with the Royal African Corps, and the creation of the West African Frontier Force over a century later.

Initially, the West India Regiments filled their ranks with enslaved men purchased by the British in the West Indies from slave ships that originated from West Africa.[33] In effect, the British Army was one of the biggest purchasers of African slaves within the West Indies.[34] By 1798, the WIR grew to a total of twelve regiments on account of continued war with France and Spain, but was reduced to only two regiments by 1819, with the numbers of regiments fluctuating in the succeeding years. The WIR's need for manpower forced British officials to look towards West Africa for "recruits." British officers believed that conscripting "liberated Africans" into the WIR from Sierra Leone would be cheaper and more efficient than either buying slaves or recruiting volunteers from the West Indies. In effect, both the RAC and WIR competed for the impressment of "liberated Africans" in Sierra Leone; but with the RAC firmly established in West Africa under the influence of colonial administrators, WIR recruiting became subordinate to that of the RAC with the WIR receiving "undesired Negroes."[35] Eventually the RAC became increasingly inefficient as an imperial military in West Africa, essentially developing into the private army of British governors of Sierra Leone, and was gradually absorbed by the WIR.

The success of the WIR in the West Indies proved to British officials that it could be used effectively to secure colonial holdings and protect British trade in West Africa. Ports and garrisons in the West Indies continued as the WIR's home bases, especially for training and recruiting purposes, but British officers devised a plan where detachments of the regiments would cycle between West Africa and the West Indies for active service. Sections of the 2nd WIR first arrived at Bathurst in 1819, when the last Royal African Corps detachments left, but departed two years later for more pressing concerns in Sierra Leone, leaving only a small detachment in the Gambia. Later, in 1831, large detachments of both the 1st and 2nd WIR returned to Bathurst to combat growing opposition from the Barra Kingdom. This incident, and a smaller punitive expedition by detachments of the 2nd and 3rd WIR in 1849, diminished the prestige of the local kingships and indirectly contributed to growing discontent among the local population that incited the Soninke-Marabout Wars.[36]

The first British intervention in the Soninke-Marabout Wars occurred in 1853. In June, Governor O'Connor led a force of about 500 soldiers of the 2nd WIR, 3rd WIR, and the Gambia Militia to invade Sabaji, pushing out the Marabouts threatening British Kombo. Again in 1855, detachments of the 2nd and 3rd WIR and the Gambia Militia advanced on Sabaji after heightened local unrest and the kidnapping of a European. However, this time they faced a much more entrenched resistance and French colonial forces from Goree were called on to help restore peace.[37] By 1860, continued unrest caused by the Soninke-Marabout Wars significantly affected British trade. The conflict not only reduced British interaction with local traders, but British stores and factories on the banks of the River Gambia were routinely raided by the warring parties. In 1861, one instance of raiding at the upriver post at Baddibu and the refusal of the local ruler to pay merchants compensation forced detachments of the 1st and 2nd WIR to depart Bathurst on a punitive expedition to Baddibu. In 1866, Amer Faal, a Marabout leader, led an attack on the British factory at Albreda. Detachments of the 4th WIR, which was recently raised for service solely in West Africa, proceeded upriver and captured Faal's compound at Tubab Kolon with cooperation from Soninke forces.[38]

After 1866, the nature of conflict in the Soninke-Marabout Wars changed and reduced direct intervention by the West India Regiments. The conflict became increasingly political with various local leaders attacking rivals for personal gain. By the 1870s, the Marabouts now ruled over the majority of the local districts in the Gambia. The Marabouts continued the conflict amongst themselves and lessened their attacks on British holdings, which influenced local rulers from surrounding areas to invade the Gambia and raid the vulnerable region. As a result, the political authority and control of Gambian rulers gradually diminished. Ultimately, the Soninke-Marabout Wars "created a power vacuum in the Gambia which the war chiefs could not, and the British authorities consistently refused to fill."[39] This situation was only rectified when the British moved to establish political control over the territory after failed attempts to do so by the French in the 1880s.

After the declaration of British colonial authority throughout the entirety of the Gambia in 1889, the mission of the WIR in the Gambia transformed into one of colonial conquest and the subjugation of the local population. In 1891, Fodi Kabba, a local chief in the Jarra districts, violently resisted British administrators and the implementation of British political control in the area of Marige, 80 kilometers west of Bathurst. A force of nearly 200 WIR soldiers advanced on Marige and destroyed it and surrounding towns, while Kabba fled to French territory. Months later, a much smaller WIR detachment was sent further upriver to Toniataba to capture Suleman Santu, Kabba's ally who also resisted the British administrators. The initial WIR detachment failed to capture Santu, but eventually a force of almost 300 WIR soldiers overran the village and killed him.[40] In 1894, an uprising of Mandingos in Kombo led by Fodi Silla, another local chief, was put down by the WIR with support from the Royal Navy, which resulted in the further destruction of Gambian villages. Like Kabba, Silla fled to French territory where he was subsequently captured by French officials.[41]

The last major punitive expedition by the West India Regiments in the Gambia occurred in the beginning of 1901 as a result of the murder of three British administrators in June 1900 in the Kiang district. Due to the drain on available troops posed by the expedition to suppress the 1900 Asante Rebellion in the Gold Coast, and the fact that no substantial WIR detachment was in the Gambia at the time of the murders, the punitive expedition had to be postponed until the required forces arrived. This delay, which put the limits of British power on display, caused a significant increase in resistance amongst the local populace to colonial authority in the Gambia. The expedition finally began on 11 January, comprising a total of over 800 soldiers from the WIR and Central African Regiment (CAR), originating from Nyasaland (today's Malawi), under the title of the "Gambia Field Force." It quickly subdued the towns of Dumbutu and Kwinella while also marching through surrounding districts as a show of force, eventually reaching the Jarra districts. The CAR, the precursor to the King's African Rifles (KAR) in British East Africa, was travelling from British Somaliland to the Gold Coast, through Gibraltar, to aid in the Asante Campaign, but was diverted to Bathurst as a result of unrest in the Gambia.[42]

The Gambia Field Force, in cooperation with the French *Tirailleurs Senegalais,* was then sent to capture Kabba and put down his rebellion near Medina, in French territory. Kabba was killed and his strongholds destroyed by 25 March 1901. The 1901 expedition was the largest and most significant British military expedition of colonial conquest in the Gambia. The Gambia Field Force killed or captured the last remaining anti-colonial fighters with significant followings, WIR and CAR soldiers visited almost every district as a show of British military power, and ultimately, the British secured colonial authority throughout the Gambia.[43]

The Gambia is a unique historical example in Africa in that British wars of colonial conquest in the Gambia were prosecuted entirely without the aid of locally raised paramilitary forces. Throughout the rest of British West Africa, local paramilitary forces, under the control of the Colonial Office, supported imperial militaries in imposing British colonial authority, while also limiting the need for imperial garrisons in such regions. The Gambia, however, raised no such local forces, until the establishment of the Gambia Company WAFF in 1902, and continually relied on temporarily garrisoned imperial militaries for defense and conquest. However, by the time the Gambia Company WAFF was established, the West India Regiments had largely succeeded in imposing British colonial authority throughout the Gambia. When the last WIR detachments departed the Gambia in 1902, the Gambia Company was left to garrison a relatively peaceful colony.

Chapter 3
The West African Frontier Force

THE ONSET OF THE SCRAMBLE FOR AFRICA and territorial competition among European powers created new military objectives for the British in West Africa. The British military in West Africa before this period was primarily concerned with the protection of trade and very small colonial enclaves like Bathurst. The West India Regiments and small locally raised constabularies or militias were largely capable of performing the mission of protecting British trade interests; however, the Scramble changed the British military imperative in West Africa to that of conquering vast swaths of territory and securing British authority in such territory against local resistance and European competition, namely from the French and eventually Germans. Beginning in 1860, the West India Regiments relied on more expensive volunteers from the West Indies rather than "liberated Africans" for recruits because the Royal Navy had essentially eliminated the Trans-Atlantic Slave Trade. In effect, British officers could no longer conscript "liberated Africans" for military service.[45] Ultimately, it was not economically feasible for the WIR to be used for the mission of colonial conquest.

As an imperial military organization, the WIR was maintained by and under the control of the War Office. If the Colonial Office required the WIR for its purposes, it needed approval and some level of cooperation from the War Office, which was at times hard to achieve. In the early stages of the Scramble, "the troops which the War Office maintained in West Africa were expected to perform strictly imperial duties."[46] This normally meant garrison and defense duties, but if they were called upon by British colonial authorities for other military operations, imperial troops were expected to execute their orders and immediately return to garrisons on the coast without engaging in "extended military operations."[47]

Additionally, maintaining an imperial military unit in West Africa with home bases on the other side of the Atlantic was extremely expensive for the British government. As members of an imperial unit of the greater British Army, WIR soldiers were entitled to the same conditions, equipment, and pay as common British soldiers—although in reality such equality was never fully achieved. Furthermore, the transport costs associated with ferrying WIR detachments not only between the West Indies and West Africa, but also between the various British West African colonies in response to crises, were both enormous and inefficient. In 1874, British officials argued that on average it cost £100 a year to maintain a WIR soldier in West Africa, while it only cost £30 a year to maintain a Hausa soldier of the local Lagos Constabulary in Nigeria.[48] Therefore, the Colonial Office sought to raise its own military forces with local soldiers to both lower costs and increase its operational control in West Africa.

In the hyper-competitive political and territorial environment that existed between European powers in Africa as a result of the Scramble, raising a much larger and cheaper military force in British West Africa provided another benefit—supporting the so-called "chess board policy." Joseph Chamberlain, the British Colonial Secretary, promoted this idea as a means to combat French encroachment on British territory in Africa. The policy dictated that placing a British garrison in certain locations, sometimes in close proximity to French garrisons, would strengthen British claims to the territory while helping combat French occupation of territory thought to be under British authority. In other words, the British needed to place military units throughout their African territories, not just in old colonial enclaves on the coast, to ensure political authority and control in the interior. Additionally, the British sought to pursue the doctrine of "effective occupation" as outlined in the 1884 Berlin Conference that defined the Scramble for Africa. The doctrine stipulated that European powers only had authority over African territory if they demonstrated occupation through local treaties and the creation of a governing administration with a police force to keep order.[49] This could not be done with relatively small and expensive WIR detachments in West Africa, nor could it be effectively achieved by small, locally raised constabularies or militias—such a policy required a force of several thousand soldiers.[50]

By the late nineteenth century, British colonial authorities had made minor strides in establishing locally raised constabulary units under the control of the Colonial Office. The Armed Hausa Police Force, later renamed the Lagos Constabulary, was one of the first to be raised in 1862 from Hausa soldiers, with the other British West African colonies raising similar forces in the succeeding decades.[51] Many of the local soldiers who served in these units were enslaved men purchased by British officers and were required to pay back this money in installments over the length of their service.[52] The Gambia is unique in British West Africa in that other than the extremely small and part-time Gambia Militia, it did not raise a paramilitary type constabulary force at all.[53]

At first, such constabulary units were only police forces that provided military services in times of crisis. Therefore, these units could not be expected to maintain garrisons and routinely participate in extended military operations in support of British territorial and colonial objectives. However, some constabularies did find themselves functioning as traditional military organizations by participating in lengthy campaigns, like the Armed Hausa Police Force during the Asante Campaign (1873-1874). By the 1890s, the constabularies had essentially evolved into military forces with training, command structures and equipment characteristic of British Army units of the time. But the same could not be said of standardization across the varying British West African forces. They lacked suitable logistical services, British officers and officials were unmotivated to improve training, and such units were often armed with outdated weapons.[54]

The West African Frontier Force was ultimately created as a means to greatly increase British military capabilities to support Colonial Office ambitions, combat continued French encroachment, and standardize and coordinate military resources across the four British West African colonies. In 1897 Chamberlain ordered the creation of the WAFF as a regular military force from the nucleus of the Royal Niger Constabulary, the armed element of the Royal Niger Company engaged in the conquest of the Nigerian hinterland which was purchased by the British government. He instructed that the force be increased by two battalions, to a strength of over 2,000 men, and that Frederick Lugard, a British officer and colonial administrator, take command of what was subsequently called the Northern Nigeria Regiment. This was necessary because of the desperate state of affairs at the time in the Nigerian hinterland—the borders between British Nigeria and the surrounding French territories had yet to be solidified and the French had advanced into the region as a result, unchecked by the 500-strong Lagos Constabulary. Regular British troops were unavailable, as many were committed in South Africa for service in the Second Anglo-Boer War (1899-1902). The massive increase in British military power achieved by creating the WAFF eventually alleviated the problem of the French territorial threat in Nigeria.[55]

From its successes in Nigeria, the Colonial Office realized the potential of a federated military force in British West Africa and noted in a June 1899 Colonial Office paper:

...this was chosen as a convenient moment to consider as a whole the position of the military forces of the Crown under the control of the Colonial Office throughout West Africa to make their forces mutually self-supporting...it was considered necessary the various constabularies and newly raised West African Frontier Force should be amalgamated into one organization and bear a military name.[56]

Chamberlain then ordered that WAFF organizations develop out of the existing local constabularies in all British West African colonies by 1899, although it was not achieved until 1902.

In effect, the West African Frontier Force absorbed the existing local constabularies led by white British military officers, but now fell under the administrative authority of the Colonial Office. Lugard was named as the first Commandant and outlined the development of the WAFF as a regional military framework. Units throughout the four colonies were to be standardized with the same equipment, training, and command structures, while an Inspector General (IG) would inspect each unit annually to ensure such standards were met. By 1902, the strength of the WAFF was over 6,500 officers and men throughout the four British West African colonies, which was a significant increase in the size of British military forces from recent years.[57] The West India Regiments presence in West Africa largely diminished after 1902, but the War Office did raise the West African Regiment (WAR) in Sierra Leone after the 1898 Hut Tax Rebellion to serve as the permanent imperial unit in the region to protect Freetown. In fact, Sierra Leone was an interesting case in that it maintained two different military organizations under the authority of different British government departments. The WAR fell under the War Office, while the Sierra Leone Battalion (SLB) of the WAFF fell under Colonial Office authority.[58] Freetown, which housed a large coaling station and port facilities for Royal Navy ships in the Atlantic, held significant imperial and strategic importance for the British, and thus, received substantial military attention, especially from the War Office.[59]

Similar to other British colonial and imperial militaries, the WAFF functioned through racial hierarchies and essentially paternalistic relationships between white British officers and black African soldiers. British officers and non-commissioned officers (NCO) were seconded from regular British Army units for short term appointments, usually around two years, to train and lead WAFF forces. Since the British served on a short-term basis in the WAFF, they rarely had the time to develop a deeper understanding, strong relationships, and overall *espirit de corps* with African soldiers. Africans were not given commissions to serve as officers, but many black soldiers did serve as NCOs to fill the language gap between the officers and men. African NCOs gradually became the bedrock of the WAFF by providing valuable experience, knowledge, and guidance for new recruits, while serving as a bridge between the officers and men in a force where the officers often knew little about the men they were leading. Such a structure did not necessarily decrease the military efficiency of the WAFF in its garrison duties or combat operations, but it did ensure that British officers were often out of touch with the social realities of their units.[60]

The social disconnect between British officers and African soldiers systematically influenced the formation and recruiting policies of West African Frontier Force units through martial race stereotypes. In recruiting for their various colonial militaries from India to West Africa, the British relied on notions of martial race theory: "the belief that some groups of men are biologically or culturally predisposed to the arts of war."[61] Such beliefs were colonial constructs based on ethnographic claims and largely invented by British officers and colonial officials; but martial race stereotypes undoubtedly influenced recruiting patterns and policies of the WAFF as British officers ensured that they targeted and recruited imagined martial races into the force rather than non-martial ones. In practice, one of the major factors in a group being labelled a "martial race" was its general acceptance of British colonial authority and "loyalty" to the British imperial cause.[62] As a result, certain groups of people in West Africa made up a disproportionate number of the WAFF rank-and-file. For example, the Hausa from northern Nigeria were initially the premier martial race in West Africa and were targeted for military recruitment. In reality, the Hausa's martial identity was invented by Europeans.

The original paramilitary forces in Nigeria, formed in the late nineteenth, were initially comprised of formerly enslaved men from the interior, who were given the generic label of "Hausa" whether they were Hausa or not. This initiated the myth that the Hausa were a martial people. However, Hausa enlistment gradually declined by the 1920s and 1930s as they found more lucrative economic opportunities elsewhere and viewed the military as an immoral institution. This forced British officers to look elsewhere in Nigeria for impoverished and marginalized communities that could fill military recruitment needs; thus, transferring the martial label to other ethnicities. Ultimately, British understandings of martial races were artificial and "based on what communities became responsive to military recruitment."[63] Although Hausa enlistment declined and martial labels shifted elsewhere, the British developed a "northern ethos" within the increasingly diverse colonial military in Nigeria based on the myth of Hausa martial status.[64]

Materialist arguments often show that groups of people were willing to be martial in British eyes for the favorable economic and social circumstances that resulted from service in colonial militaries.[65] Ultimately, men enlisted for such socioeconomic benefits, which informed the British of which communities to label as "martial." This pattern affected military recruitment in the Gambia. Similarly, Mende men were the imagined martial race of Sierra Leone, but later became non-martial in British eyes. Mende men initially formed the majority of the rank-and-file of the Gambia Company, but recruiting patterns and martial labels soon transitioned to the Serahule and Bambara peoples of the Senegambia region, with small numbers of other ethnic groups also represented in the company.[66]

The West African Frontier Force maintained distinct differences with the French West African colonial army, the *Tirailleurs Senegalais*. The WAFF was not envisioned as an imperial army for use outside of West Africa. It had a strictly colonial mission to "maintain internal security, defend the territorial frontiers, and provide aid when required for neighboring colonies."[67] Ultimately, the WAFF was founded on the principles of "efficiency and economy," where deploying the force for military operations outside of West Africa would surely negate such principles and require the creation of a much larger and more expensive force than intended. Additionally, the WAFF was under Colonial Office control and funded by the respective colonial governments; so, it was inconceivable for the Gambia colonial government to fund a military expedition in the farthest reaches of the British Empire.

On the contrary, the *Tirailleurs Senegalais*, formed in 1857, was intended to be an imperial army for service within West Africa and beyond. Similar to the WAFF, the *Tirailleurs Senegalais* functioned through racial hierarchies between European officers and African soldiers, while recruiting policies were based on notions of martial races.[68] However, the *Tirailleurs* often fought alongside regular French soldiers during various conflicts, to include the Western Front in Europe during the First World War. The greatest influence behind such a phenomenon in the French colonial military was French military officer Charles Mangin and his idea of *La Force Noire*.

In 1910 Mangin noted "first, that black Africa was an almost inexhaustible reservoir of men, and second, that by nature and history these men were ideally suited for military service."[69] He argued for the exploitation of France's colonial holdings in West Africa for manpower to supply a large imperial army, while this imperial army could eventually replace French soldiers and execute France's military objectives in Europe, Africa, and elsewhere. In the most shocking of colonial ideologies, Mangin ultimately argued for the creation of such a force to save the lives of white French soldiers in warfare, especially in a period of declining French birthrates and the increasing German military threat, viewing African soldiers as expendable for imperial purposes. Mangin's views indirectly influenced French efforts to expand the *Tirailleurs Senegalais* through universal conscription beginning in 1912, during both times of peace and conflict, which gave the French the most substantial military resources in colonial West Africa.[70]

Mangin's views made some headway within British military circles concerning the West African Frontier Force and other British-led African colonial militaries. The "Million Black Army Movement" among some British officials came as a result of the First World War and the ghastly casualty rates experienced on the Western Front. Like Mangin, some British officials argued that African soldiers could augment British forces in Europe or elsewhere to replace casualties and increase British military strength. However, the Colonial Office continually resisted the use of African soldiers outside of Africa, especially against European soldiers, by arguing that "African soldiers had lower levels of training, would not survive in temperate climates, and were generally unreliable."[71]

Such views ensured that the WAFF was confined to the African continent during the First World War and was only reluctantly sent to Southeast Asia during the Second World War to fight a non-European opponent. Contrasting the British and French imperial mindsets surrounding their West African colonial militaries shows that the WAFF was founded on the premise that it was a strictly colonial organization. Its primary mission was colonial defense and security to promote British authority in West Africa. The WAFF was only used for imperial purposes outside of West Africa in response to dire circumstances within the British Empire. In other words, the British did not form, nor did they initially intend to use, the WAFF as an African Imperial Army.

Chapter 4
The Formation and Early Years of the Gambia Company

ON 9 DECEMBER, 1901, Captain C.O. Graham, seconded from the Royal Marines, with three other British officers and two British NCOs landed at Bathurst with orders to form a West African Frontier Force company of 120 men for defense of the Gambia. They were instructed to form one quarter of the company from Gambian recruits, with the rest of the men obtained in Sierra Leone from the Sierra Leone Battalion. On 12 December, Captain Graham enlisted the first Gambian recruits, and by the end of the month the company had grown to a strength of 30 men.

With the 30 soldiers training at the company's newly established camp at Kwinella, Captain Graham travelled to Sierra Leone to gather the rest of his men. Upon arrival, Captain Graham was surprised to find that not much was known about the Gambia Company's formation among officials in Sierra Leone, and the trained soldiers required to form the nucleus of the Gambia Company were not available. As a result, Captain Graham was forced to enlist untrained recruits, who were offset by only "a few trained men" from the SLB. Throughout the month of January 1902, the Sierra Leonean recruits arrived at Bathurst and joined the local recruits for training at Kwinella. By 2 February, the Gambia Company reached its full strength of 120 men, continuing to train regularly. In June, the Gambia Company was officially recognized as an independent unit of the WAFF separate from the SLB.[72]

The British position in the Gambia at the time explains why the Gambia Company was formed from a nucleus of Sierra Leonean recruits. As noted, no constabulary force existed in the Gambia from which the Gambia Company could be formed. Other British West African colonies formed their WAFF units from the already present constabularies with sufficiently trained soldiers and British officers. It should be noted that it was a well-established practice to create colonial militaries from a nucleus of men that did not originate from the territory the military was to be garrisoned. For example, the early British colonial militaries in East Africa (Kenya) initially maintained large numbers of Sudanese soldiers. This is largely because in the early stages of colonial encroachment into these regions, the British had yet to establish sustainable recruiting relations with local communities.[73] The Gambia, however, only had a militia of citizen soldiers—regular Bathurst townspeople who could not serve as professional soldiers—and the departing detachments of the West India Regiments.[74] Therefore, the small number of local recruits needed to be offset with trained Sierra Leonean soldiers in order to form a functional military unit; but, as it turned out, such trained Sierra Leoneans were extremely sparse at the time of the company's formation.[75]

Although the British had long-standing relations with the local Gambian communities and a well-established colonial enclave at Bathurst, full colonial authority had only recently been consolidated in the interior along the River Gambia. This meant that the British lacked any deep-rooted relationship with communities that could serve as a valuable source of recruits. In other words, the British had yet to find a "martial race" in the Gambia from which they could draw effective and "loyal" soldiers.

British officials argued that "the idea of not enlisting too large a proportion of local men was based on the supposition that in the event of trouble they might throw in their lot with their own kith and kin."[76] Clearly, fears over Gambian disloyalty influenced sustained recruitment of Sierra Leoneans for service in the Gambia. With over half of the company's strength consisting of Mende and Temne soldiers, the largest ethnic groups of Sierra Leone, the British believed that trained Sierra Leoneans could help establish a high degree of military competence and tradition in the new unit. The territorial question surrounding the Gambia played a role as well. British colonial control of the Gambia was initially viewed as a means to exchange for territory with the French elsewhere in West Africa.[77] Although it was not explicitly mentioned by British officials, the use of Sierra Leonean soldiers in the Gambia would not represent a waste of resources should the Gambia eventually fall under French control. Such soldiers could easily be repatriated to Sierra Leone and continue their service with the Sierra Leone Battalion, while the British would not have wasted extensive resources in training and equipping a large force of Gambian recruits. The British slowly developed the Gambia Company into an all-Gambian force after they realized that a territorial exchange was unlikely, as well as recognizing the need to create a local reserve, and reduce the continued expense of transporting men between Sierra Leone and the Gambia. Gambian military recruitment was somewhat difficult owing to better economic opportunities in the Gambia compared to Sierra Leone. By the time of the First World War, only half of the company were local recruits.[78]

The British colonial military in the Gambia was unique in that the British decided to raise only one infantry company of 120 men in the Gambia.[79] The other West African Frontier Force units throughout British West Africa were much larger, in either battalion strength (Sierra Leone) or comprised of multiple battalions (the Gold Coast Regiment and the Northern and Southern Nigeria Regiments). A British battalion usually consisted of 500 to 800 men. Of course, the Gambia was the smallest colony, and such a small territory did not necessarily need a massive British military presence. However, there was a precedent of large British military contingents in the Gambia, as the 1901 punitive expedition consisted of over 800 soldiers.[80] More to the point was the general acceptance of British colonial authority within the Gambia among both the locals and neighboring French officials. Historian Edho Ekoko argued that the formation of WAFF units was based on the political climate of the colony; where "once effective occupation had been demonstrated, a measure of administrative machinery established and as soon as the local population began to show signs of cooperation, the tendency was to cut down the army."[81]

In 1901, the West India Regiments and the Central African Regiment effectively destroyed the last substantial resistance to colonial authority among Gambians. Additionally, the French had officially recognized British control of the River Gambia and its surrounding territory since 1889. Therefore, there were no substantial internal or external threats to British authority in the Gambia that the WAFF would need to meet with a large military response. The formation of one infantry company was sufficient to meet the colonial defense and internal security needs of the Gambia and promote British authority in the territory.

During the early months of 1902, the new Gambia Company continued its training at Kwinella until 16 April, when it was tasked with its first mission. The company joined a company of the WIR, which was still stationed in the Gambia until the Gambia Company was sufficiently trained, and marched to the town of Bita in the Foni District for a punitive expedition against the inhabitants of the town for resistance to British authority. Governor George Denton accompanied the expedition, which was a success for the British who suffered no casualties while Bita and some surrounding villages were burned as a show of force.

On 31 May, the last remaining WIR company left Bathurst and a Gambia Company detachment took up the vacant positions defending the town. On several occasions in the following years, Gambia Company detachments accompanied the governor, or other colonial officials, on tours of the colony and conducted small punitive expeditions to collect taxes or punish criminals. By 1903, the Gambia Company's fortified positions were complete. Company headquarters were moved from Kwinella to Bathurst, a more effective camp was constructed at Cape St. Mary, and permanent defensive posts on the coast and surrounding Bathurst were established. However, no such defensive posts were established in the interior of the colony largely because there was no substantial Gambian resistance to British rule and the French had already recognized the Gambia's borders.[82]

Although the British formed the Gambia Company around a small cohort of trained and experienced soldiers from Sierra Leone, the company still suffered substantial discipline and control problems in its first couple of years. In December 1902, there was an apparent mutiny among the soldiers demanding extra pay. It was quickly put down, but some of the mutineers' demands were met. Although they gained no increase in pay, they obtained additional "subsistence money" offered by the governor and better accommodation for the company.[83] Previously, the company occupied the small and dilapidated structures that once housed the WIR, while married men of the company were forced to find housing in Bathurst. British officials agreed to the construction of new barracks for the company, which was not completed until 1908.[84] Additionally, flogging would not be used as a punishment in the Gambia. At the time, although corporal punishment had been banned in the metropolitan British Army since the 1880s, flogging was a common punishment throughout British colonial militaries, especially the WAFF. However, no mention of it exists in Gambia Company documents and none of the mutineers received the punishment.[85] The ringleaders were largely lower ranking members of the company; eleven men were discharged from the company, three of whom were imprisoned, while the Company Sergeant Major (CSM) was demoted to Sergeant.[86]

Mutinous behavior was not a new phenomenon among African soldiers of British colonial militaries at the time of the Gambia Mutiny. Viewing themselves as laborers within a colonial institution, African soldiers used mutinies as a legitimate means to protest against poor conditions of service and broken contracts[87] In some instances mutinies were rather successful in helping the soldiers achieve concessions, and rarely were they violent. The Gambia Mutiny, however, may have had external influences in its creation. The Gambia Company had recently served alongside a company of the WIR on a punitive expedition in April 1902, an interaction that surely exposed the soldiers of the Gambia Company to the inequalities in conditions of service that existed between the WIR and the WAFF. WIR soldiers were entitled to better conditions of service due to their imperial designation compared to colonial soldiers of the WAFF.[88] Historian S.C. Ukpabi argued:

> *...the employment of West Indian Negro troops and the conditions of service which they were given were considered by the colonial governors as setting a bad example for the local troops, who were raised and paid negligible wages while at the same time being used for all manner of service. These governors feared that the local troops, through their association with the West Indian troops, pick up 'bad habits' and even agitate to be given the same treatment and conditions of service as West Indians.*[89]

No matter the influences, the Gambia Mutiny of 1902 proved that the Gambia Company still needed substantial development, in terms of discipline and organization, before it would become an efficient military organization.

Most of that development fell on the shoulders of the African NCOs of the company, who were initially not trusted by Captain Graham. In June 1904, Graham noted "I have been handicapped considerably in having hardly any native NCOs who can be trusted in the least so that the work devolves more on the British NCOs than would happen otherwise."[90] Part of this outlook could have stemmed from the mutiny in 1902, but such a comment shows that the individuals tasked to be a bridge between the British officers and African soldiers had yet to gain the necessary experience to be successful in this role. Brigadier General G.V. Kemball, IG of the WAFF, observed the deficiencies among the African NCOs of the company in 1904 and noted:

> *The native Non-commissioned Officers do not seem to me to have much influence with the men, or to be in proper touch with the Officers and British Non-commissioned Officers, otherwise I think that the men's complaints would have been brought to notice in a proper manner, and a settlement arrived at, without the bad feeling recently shown. At present, the Company is, in my opinion, managed too much through the British Non-commissioned Officers, and I think it will be better in the future for the Officers to have more direct dealing with the Native ranks and to find means of increasing the responsibility and influence of the native Non-commissioned Officers.*[91]

However, credit must be given to the African NCOs for the monumental task placed before them. Their language skills, military experience, and familiarity with local customs and culture were supposed to help facilitate effective military training within the Gambia Company. Such a task is extremely hard when the company is composed of men from seventeen different ethnicities and three separate colonies—Sierra Leone, the Gambia, and surrounding French territory—with each ethnicity usually having their own language and culture. The Gambia Company surely was not a homogenous group and it would take time for the African NCOs to establish effective authority and control over the diverse group of men. Additionally, the company was only recently established. Therefore, it would take time for the NCOs themselves to develop the necessary military experience and expertise required for their positions.[92]

By 1906, Captain Graham recognized a considerable improvement among the African NCOs: "I am finding that generally speaking, the NCOs are beginning to have a more real authority and in consequence I am beginning to feel that I can entrust them with work and responsibility which some time ago I would only have entrusted to a European."[93] He noted that such improvement was the result of NCOs associating themselves with higher classes of Bathurst society and viewing themselves "as above the position of a private in the Force."[94] Although this hierarchical based argument might be partly true by helping the NCOs gain confidence and status to serve as intermediaries within the company, it was probably more the process of NCOs getting to know the men they were leading and gaining valuable experience that resulted in their increased efficiency.

Nonetheless, the situation shows the importance that British officers placed on African NCOs within the West African Frontier Force. Without their leadership, the British could not achieve effective levels of discipline, training, and organization. The situation also shows how British officials preferred African NCOs to British NCOs for service in the WAFF, largely because of social and linguistic reasons and the fact that African NCOs received substantially less pay. In fact, British NCOs were often a source of discontent among African NCOs. The presence of British NCOs often undermined the authority of African NCOs, while the differing conditions of service between them strengthened perceptions of racial inequalities within the WAFF.[95] Because of racial hierarchies, all white soldiers, no matter what rank, held authority over black soldiers. This was particularly problematic within the NCO ranks where British NCOs felt superior to African NCOs despite the fact that they held the same or inferior rank. By 1906, Captain Graham was confident in the company's African NCOs and reduced the number of British NCOs serving with the Gambia Company by two.[96]

The Gambia Company was still not a homogenous group, and colonial recruiting policies continued to create a sustained dependency on Sierra Leone for new recruits. After the initial batch of recruits from Sierra Leone in 1902, when Captain Graham personally travelled to Freetown, recruiting in Sierra Leone was out of the hands of Gambia Company officers. Sierra Leonean recruits intended for the Gambia Company were selected by British officers of the Sierra Leone Battalion without input from officers in the Gambia.[97] As a result, a trend developed where the Gambia Company received recruits largely unwanted by the SLB, due to poor performance or discipline. Governor Denton even noted that such Sierra Leonean soldiers "were not as good as the local men."[98]

Additionally, Gambia Company officers did not know the backgrounds of the men they received from Sierra Leone or elsewhere. For example, Lance Corporal Theophilus Benjamin joined the company in 1904. However, before serving with the Gambia Company, Lance Corporal Benjamin served as a private in the West African Regiment under the alias of Massa Williams and took part in the Asante Expedition before being discharged for "ignominy."[99] Although it is not confirmed, he most likely participated in the WAR mutiny of 1901 and was discharged as a result.[100] Lance Corporal Benjamin served with distinction in the Gambia Company, but his case shows the bureaucratic disconnect that often existed between the War Office and Colonial Office in their handling of their respective militaries in West Africa, causing recruiting for them to be haphazard, especially in the Gambia's case.[101]

Recruits from Sierra Leone continued to largely comprise Mendes and Temnes, the largest ethnic groups of Sierra Leone, but such noted trends influenced an ideological shift among officers in the Gambia where they now viewed certain ethnicities of the Senegambia region as more martial and better soldiers than the once perceived martial races of Sierra Leone. In 1908, British officials argued to increase the recruitment of local soldiers, but due to continued fears of disloyalty, the number of local soldiers was only increased to half the strength of the company.[102]

As martial race hierarchies developed between Sierra Leonean and Gambian recruits, similar hierarchies developed among the locals of Senegambia. In 1903, Captain Graham stated that he preferred the recruitment of Wolofs from Senegal. However, the number of Wolofs in the company never rose to more than six individuals throughout the Gambia Company's early years.[103] In 1908, Mandingos were noted to "make very good soldiers," but like Wolofs, Mandingos never made up a large number of recruits.[104] Rather, personnel figures show that the Bambara and Serahule made up the majority of local recruits. The Bambara were explicitly stated as being "exceptionally good men" and effective soldiers throughout various annual reports, being specifically targeted for recruitment by British officers; but the Bambara largely originated from surrounding French territory at great distances from Bathurst.[105] In fact, the Bambara, like the Wolofs, were also considered a martial race by the French and preferred for recruitment into the *Tirailleurs Senegalais*. The British wanted Bambara recruits because they admired the military efficiency of the *Tirailleurs Senegalais* and hoped to develop the same type of military identity in the Gambia Company. In essence, the British attempted to copy French military recruiting patterns.[106]

However, it is less clear why the Serahule made up such a large proportion of local recruits, at times more than the Bambara. There are no specific mentions in reports of martial qualities among the Serahule and targeted recruitment by the British until 1926.[107] It could bethat the Serahule were the most readily available for recruitment in the Gambia, originating within Gambian territory, as opposed to the Bambara originating from French territory. Morelikely, the Serahule were in a transitional stage of economic development, leading them to accept military service for socioeconomic advancement within colonial society.[108] The Serahule are also associated with the Soninke, who were defeated in the Soninke-Marabout Wars, and served as mercenaries during the conflict for Soninke leaders.[109] Their defeat placed the Serahule at a socioeconomic disadvantage within Gambian society, which service in the Gambia Company helped remedy. It is worth noting that the majority of local recruits from Gambian territory often came from upriver and not from Bathurst, which supports the trend that imagined martial races originated from remote and marginalized areas.

Although the Bambara and Serahule formed the majority of local recruits, small numbers of Mandingos, Wolofs, Fulas, Tukulors, and other ethnicities from the Gambia and surrounding French territory were recruited into the Gambia Company.[110] Eventually, after the First World War, when the Gambia Company essentially became an all-Gambian force of local recruits, eighteen different ethnicities were represented in the ranks with Fula constituting the greatest number of soldiers.[111] These patterns show the fluidity and artificiality surrounding British understandings of martial races.

Such recruiting patterns of both Sierra Leonean and local recruits ultimately diminished the efficiency of the Gambia Company as an independent unit by ensuring that the effective formation of a reserve force of discharged soldiers was impossible to accomplish. In 1904, British officials made substantial efforts to establish reserve forces throughout the West African Frontier Force.[112] This was extremely important for the Gambia Company, because should the company find itself in a large and sustained conflict, the reserves could be called up to strengthen its already small military position in the Gambia and replace casualties. Otherwise, the Gambia Company would essentially cease to exist, a prominent fear among Gambia Company officers during the First World War.

However, recruiting policies of the Gambia Company systematically ensured that no reserve force could develop. First, Sierra Leonean recruits were repatriated to Sierra Leone after their service with the Gambia Company. The soldiers had a choice to remain in the Gambia and join the Gambia Company reserve, but it appears that nearly every soldier opted to return home and join the reserve force of the Sierra Leone Battalion. The second drain on the Gambia Company reserve were local recruits from French territory. Similarly, these soldiers returned to French territory upon completion of their service and could not be called upon as reservists by British authorities as a result.[113] In fact, there was a trend among local recruits where they would serve in the company long enough to earn a good amount of money and subsequently desert to French territory.

Captain Graham noted that "they feel a certain feeling of independence and consequently desert if at any time they are tired of the work."[114] Between 1904 and 1914, there were fifty-six desertions recorded.[115] This not only decreased the company's ability to form an effective reserve, but also decreased the efficiency of the company itself through soldiers deserting to French territory with little chance of punishment. The last drain on the Gambia Company's reserve was local competition. The small number of soldiers who originated from within Gambian borders often preferred more lucrative opportunities upon completion of their service, like service in the Gambia Police Force, rather than signing up for the Gambia Company reserve. Such local labor competition also limited the number of recruits the Gambia Company could obtain from in and around Bathurst in the first place. Brigadier General P.S. Wilkinson, Inspector General of the WAFF, noted this was due "to the high rate of wages obtainable in Bathurst."[116] The situation was so bad that in 1913, there was only one reservist listed on the Gambia Company roster.[117]

Despite its shortcomings, the Gambia Company did produce valuable results in its early years. From 1902 until the onset of the First World War, there was no large-scale resistance to British authority in the Gambia. As noted, detachments of the Gambia Company routinely accompanied colonial officials on tours of the colony and met small acts of colonial resistance with force. Such expeditions were apparently enough to dissuade any continued resistance among Gambians.[118] Furthermore, the company made strides in the military development of its rank-and-file. A school was established where soldiers learned English and technical skills like signaling, while the company kept up to date on training by incorporating approved WAFF tactics, especially bush fighting, into its regimen at Cape St. Mary. Throughout this period the company maintained its status as being "fit for active service" within the Gambia and elsewhere in West Africa.[119]

In 1913, the company was rearmed with Short Magazine Lee Enfield (SMLE) Mk III rifles, a notable improvement from its previous armament of the Magazine Lee Enfield (MLE) and the Lee Enfield Carbine. Throughout its early years, the Gambia Company also maintained two 6-pounder quick firing Hotchkiss guns positioned in defense of Bathurst. However, the guns were decommissioned in 1913 due to their age and never replaced because of the expense required to procure and operate new guns. British officials ultimately viewed the guns as unnecessary in the Gambia to defend against any attack by locals, as appropriate amounts of force could be supplied by the Gambia Company and the Gambia Police.[120] Lastly, by 1914 the strength of the company gradually increased to about 130 Africans, half of whom were local recruits, and five British, although arguments were made to increase the strength by an additional fourteen men for an artillery detachment which never formed.[121]

Section One Conclusion

TRACING ITS EARLY DEVELOPMENT exposes how unique the Gambia Company was in relation to the greater West African Frontier Force. It operated in a territory largely unwanted by British colonial officials and was given a relatively easy task owing to the fact that previous imperial militaries secured British colonial authority in the Gambia, which subsequently lacked any continued resistance. However, recruiting policies ensured that the company's effectiveness in potential sustained military operations was limited, as it was unable to create and sustain a reserve force. The Gambia Company's early years were marked by setbacks, but also substantial progress. As a small independent unit of the WAFF with no direct predecessor, the Gambia Company was essentially formed out of thin air, but established enough military competency to effectively carry out its mission in the Gambia and remain eligible for active service elsewhere. Such progress created a strong foundation which the Gambia Company relied upon during the First World War.

Section Two

The Gambia Company during the First World War, 1914-1918

THE FIRST WORLD WAR is well-known as the first instance of modern industrialized warfare, creating massive devastation along the Western Front and elsewhere in Europe. However, the conflict brought proportionally as much devastation, if not more, to Africa where European powers used the continent as a battleground to achieve individual imperial objectives. At the onset of war, Germany held four colonies throughout Sub-Saharan Africa—Togoland (today's Togo and parts of Ghana), Cameroon (today's Republic of Cameroon and a small part of Nigeria), German South-West Africa (today's Namibia), and German East Africa (today's Burundi, Rwanda, and mainland Tanzania). For strategic purposes, the Allied powers sought to capture German naval facilities and destroy wireless communications stations in these colonies. However, such strategic objectives soon turned into excuses for territorial conquest. The Allies ultimately sought to eliminate Germany's colonial claims in Africa while enlarging their own empires on the continent. The First World War was essentially the last phase of the "Scramble for Africa."[1]

Caught up in the conflict were ordinary Africans. They either served as soldiers or carriers, who were commonly employed in West African warfare as logistical support, in European-led colonial militaries or watched as such militaries ravaged their homelands. Ultimately, no part of the continent was spared from this devastating conflict, with tiny Gambia as a case in point. The Gambia and the Gambia Company took up their imperial obligations by supplying men for active service in some of the farthest reaches of the continent and in some of the most crucial moments of the African campaigns.

The Gambia Company underwent an interesting evolution during the First World War. Despite its small size and independence relative to the greater West African Frontier Force, the Gambia Company transformed from a unit incapable of carrying out its primary task of colonial defense to a battle-hardened group of soldiers willing to go toe-to-toe in combat with the locally raised German colonial military, the *Schutztruppe*.[2]

The Gambia Company was employed and provided valuable service in both the Cameroon and East Africa campaigns. Furthermore, there were unique strains placed on the Gambia in order to fulfill its imperial responsibilities in time of war. The Gambia, being the smallest British colony in Africa, maintained the same obligations as its much larger sister colonies, to include supplying the Gambia Company as part of the WAFF for active service elsewhere on the continent. The Gambian government needed to ensure that such a commitment did not leave the colony defenseless nor place a relatively unfair burden on its inhabitants. Analyzing the Gambia and the Gambia Company during the First World War is surely an extremely narrow lens on a much wider conflict, but such an analysis helps uncover some of the lowest level dynamics that shaped the conflict in Africa.

Chapter 5
War is Declared

LIKE IN MANY PLACES, THE DECLARATION OF WAR in 1914 brought uncertainty and fear to the Gambia. The Gambia was the smallest British colony in Africa with only one infantry company defending it, so it was perceived, mainly by the residents of Bathurst, as the most vulnerable colony to enemy attack. In November, Gambian insecurity manifested itself when a British cruiser, *H.M.S Highflyer*, approaching the Gambia River was wrongly identified as a German cruiser. The inhabitants believed that the ship would bombard Bathurst as the Gambia Company, without any artillery support, would be unable to stop German forces from taking over the colony.[3] These fears were driven more by nervousness than anything else, as both the Colonial Office and the British Navy maintained the belief that the Gambia offered no strategic value to the Germans.

Additionally, the German naval threat was nonexistent in West Africa. In August, three German cruisers—the *Dresden*, *Eber*, and *Panther*—were in West African waters, but fled towards South America upon hearing the news of war. After August 1914, there were reports they were still in the area, but these were unfounded.[4] The only significant German naval threat to Allied positions in Sub-Saharan Africa was the *Konigsberg* in the Indian Ocean near German East Africa. However, the German cruiser *Emden* did bombard the Indian port city of Madras in September 1914, so fears of the Germans bombarding Bathurst were not entirely irrational.[5] Ultimately, the Anglo-French wartime alliance ensured that the Gambia would receive military support from surrounding French West Africa in the event of crisis.[6]

However, the event reveals how the Gambia Company, at the outbreak of war, was inadequately prepared in its purpose of defending the Gambia colony. The company recently disposed of two "ancient" Hotchkiss machine guns and relied on one "very old and inaccurate" Maxim gun, while the Gambia Company lacked any artillery capability.[7] All that was available to defend the Gambia against a potential German attack was the company's roughly 130 men armed with rifles, supported by a small police force. There was no effective reserve force, while many experienced members of the company had recently retired after completing twelve years of service (since the founding of the company) and were replaced by new recruits.[8] Twelve years of service was the standard enlistment period for African colonial soldiers necessary to earn veteran benefits. Gambian fears were certainly warranted as the Gambia Company was woefully underprepared for any potential German attack in August 1914.

The Gambia Company received notice of war on 4 August, however, defensive measures in the colony had been initiated on 30 July. Each British colony was supplied with a Defense Scheme to outline how the colony would be defended by its resident colonial military forces in the event of war. The Gambia Defense Scheme emphasized a potential landing by enemy forces on the small Gambian coast, most likely in the vicinity of Bathurst. In cooperation with the Gambia Police, the Gambia Company positioned itself for the defense of the colony's most important town, largely leaving the rest of the colony undefended. Bathurst was divided into four districts, with each district assigned guard patrols. A lookout was posted at Barra Point, opposite Bathurst on the River Gambia, while entrenchments were constructed in the vicinity of Oyster Creek, west of Bathurst, to protect the only bridge connecting the town to the mainland. Company detachments assigned at these various posts were cycled out weekly, while training continued at the company's camp at Cape St. Mary.[9]

In addition to its defense responsibilities in the Gambia, the fact that the Gambia Company formed part of the West African Frontier Force made it liable for active service elsewhere. With the formal declaration of war on 5 August, the WAFF "was placed under the conditions of active service," meaning that the Gambia Company awaited orders to support imperial defense outside of the Gambia, should it be needed.[10] At the outbreak of war, Germany held two colonies in West Africa—Togoland and Cameroon. Togoland housed an important wireless transmitter which connected Germany's African colonies and Atlantic-based ships to Berlin. In the span of roughly two weeks, the Gold Coast Regiment (GCR) of the WAFF and the French-led *Tirailleurs Senegalais* destroyed the transmitter and took over the colony with relative ease.[11] However, tackling Cameroon proved to be a more difficult task for the Allies, due to the territory's greater size, more arduous terrain, and a larger German colonial military establishment. As a result, the campaign required the service of all available WAFF units, to include the Gambia Company.

Objectives in Cameroon ultimately differed among the Allies. In 1911,

France ceded over 250,000 square kilometers of Central African territory to Cameroon in return for German recognition of French acquisitions in Morocco. The French intended to recover this ceded territory. Therefore, the French invaded Cameroon with the objective of territorial conquest.[12] The British, however, were not concerned with conquest, at least initially. Much like the wireless transmitter in Togoland, Cameroon housed a wireless transmitter at Duala. Reports indicated that this wireless station was jamming British naval communications in the Atlantic, while German officials were still receiving messages from Berlin with the help of another transmitter located on the nearby Spanish island of Fernando Po. Duala also maintained valuable port facilities that serviced German naval cruisers and supply vessels. With the fall of Togoland, Duala was the last German naval station in West Africa that could resupply ships headed south from Europe towards Germany's two other African colonies—German South West and East Africa.[13] Therefore, the initial British motivation for invading Cameroon was maritime while the French motivation was territorial.

On 10 September, the first detachment of the Gambia Company, a signaling unit of sixteen men, left the Gambia for active operations in Cameroon. Another two British officers, including the commanding officer of the company, Captain V.B. Thurston, fifty rank-and-file, and seven machine gun carriers left the colony on 15 January 1915. The last Gambia Company detachment left Bathurst on 14 September, bringing the Gambia contingent in Cameroon to full company strength. The staggered deployment to Cameroon ensured that the company's defensive responsibilities were not abandoned outright before suitable replacements could be formed and trained. However, there was not enough time to form a substantial reserve component for the Gambia Company, so the burden fell on the Gambia Police to guard the colony.[14]

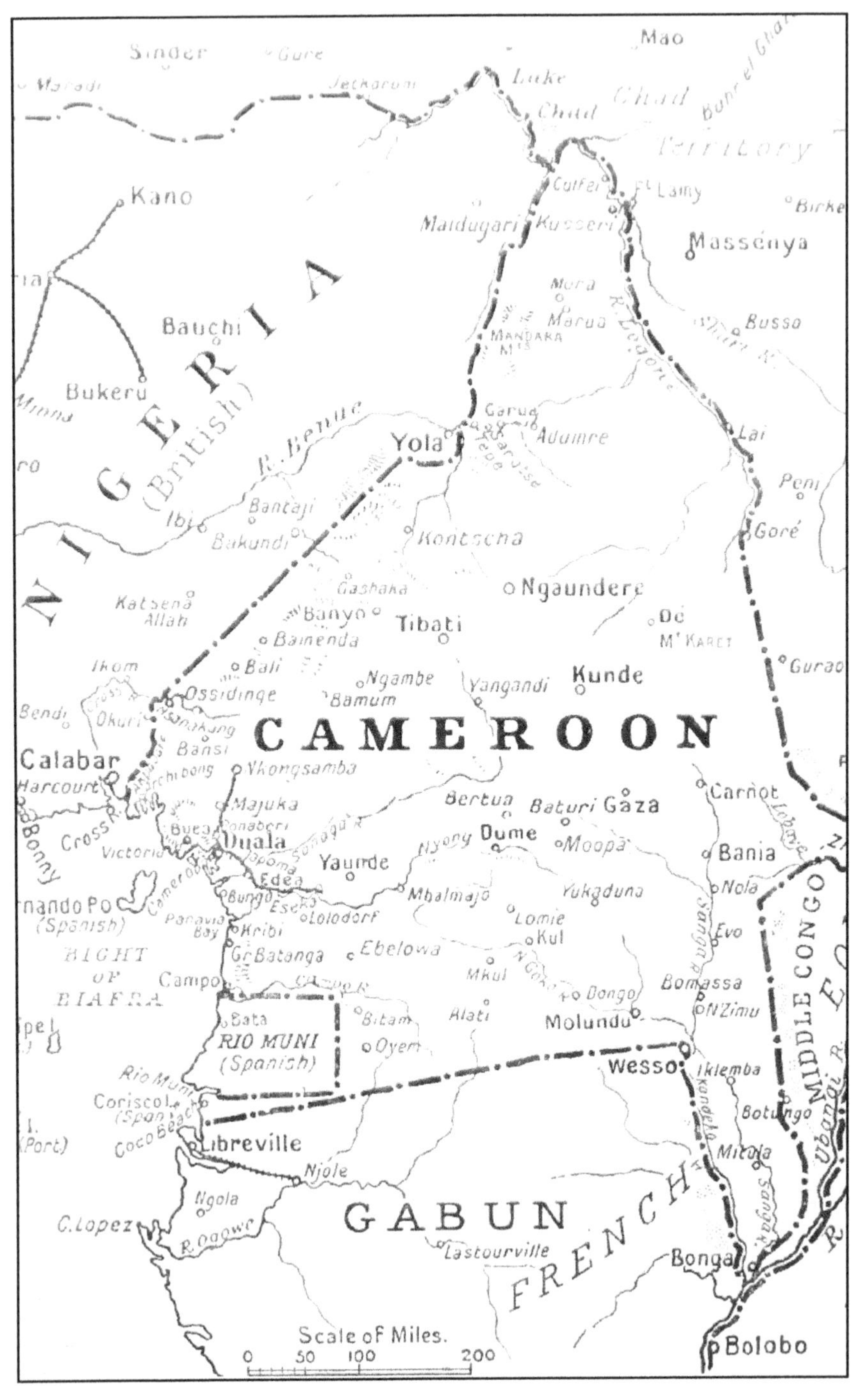

NIGERIA (British)
CAMEROON
GABUN
FRENCH
MIDDLE CONGO
RIO MUNI (Spanish)
Kano
Bauchi
Bukeru
Yola
Calabar
Duala
Yaunde
Libreville
Ngaundere
Tibati
Kunde
Lake Chad
Chad Territory
Ft Lamy
Massénya
Maidugari
Kusseri
Garua
Gaza
Dume
Bania
Wesso
Molundu
Bonga
Bolobo
Njole
C. Lopez
Lastourville
Fernando Po (Spanish)
BIGHT OF BIAFRA
Scale of Miles.
0 50 100 200

Chapter 6
Operations in Cameroon

KARL EBERMAIER, GOVERNOR OF GERMAN CAMEROON, initially announced that his colony sought to remain neutral in a European war based on the Congo Act of 1885. The act stated that European powers could proclaim neutrality for their colonial holdings in equatorial Africa, more specifically the Congo Basin area, to preserve colonial integrity. In reality, the Allies had no intention of respecting Cameroon's neutrality, while the Germans had no expectation that they would.[15] Only one third of German Cameroon fell within the designated Congo Basin area; but beyond that, Germany herself broke the Congo Act when German columns attacked Belgian troops near the Ubangi River from German East Africa on 28 August 1914.[16] This brought Belgium into the Cameroon campaign in support of the French and British, ultimately making the Cameroon campaign a truly Allied effort.

The German military strategy rested on protracted defense of Cameroon to "ensure that when the hostilities in Europe came to an end Germany's claim to the colony would, at the peacetalks, still be bolstered by possession."[17] They viewed the interior of the colony, the central and northern plateau of Cameroon, as the most naturally defendable area where the outnumbered and poorly supplied *Schutztruppe* could endure against Allied forces. In the northern portion of the colony a "line of mountains, parallel with the Nigerian frontier, formed a plateau, covered in tall elephant grass, free of the tsetse fly, and favourable to livestock;" while in the southern portion of the colony lay jungle and swamp with numerous rivers that made military maneuvers extremely difficult and brought disease to humans and animals alike.[18] Therefore, to ensure their strategy of protracted resistance, the Germans positioned themselves in the more favorable regions of the colony and, in effect, gave the Allies free rein within the more onerous regions in southern Cameroon.

The German strategy conveniently supported the initial Allied motivations for invasion—it allowed the British to seize the maritime objectives at Duala and the French to obtain their territorial objectives in the east. Ultimately, the loss of Duala or territory in the east did not hurt Germany's strategic position in Cameroon's interior. The Germans centered their defensive strategy on Ngaundere, in the interior of the colony, with large *Schutztruppe* garrisons at towns such as Yaunde and Garua, which left Duala essentially defenseless. Erroneously, the Allies assumed that the Germans would prioritize defenses around Duala and leave much weaker *Schutztruppe* garrisons in the northern portions of the colony.[19] At the outbreak of war, the *Schutztruppe* in Cameroon numbered 185 European and over 1,500 Africans. Additionally, there was an armed police force of thirty Europeans and 1,500 Africans. By the end of the campaign, over 10,000 individuals had fought on the German side as European reservists were called up and substantial numbers of locals were recruited.[20]

The Nigeria Defense Scheme, which emphasized the territorial threat from German Cameroon along its roughly 2,500-kilometer border with Nigeria, ultimately initiated the British invasion of the colony. It called for the creation of four columns at Maiduguri, Yola, Ikom and Calabar for defensive purposes against a potential German invasion. However, those columns were quickly used for offensive purposes in support of the Allied amphibious landing at Duala. Colonel C.H.P Carter, commandant of the Nigerian Regiment WAFF, believed that an attack on the *Schutztruppe* garrisons at Mora and Garua would divert German military and manpower resources away from Duala and allow the Allies an easier seaborne invasion of the town. Additionally, imagined British successes at Mora and Garua would free up WAFF soldiers stationed on the Cameroon border to support Allied advances on Duala. However, Carter did not know that the Germans had substantially reinforced their northern garrisons with *Schutztruppe* forces from the south, which made such garrisons much stronger than anticipated.[21]

By 20 August, Colonel Carter's columns crossed the border into Cameroon, but were soon met with disaster. At Mora, Garua, and Nsanakang the British found much stronger *Schutztruppe* emplacements than they expected and were unable to capture any of the towns apart from minor surrounding outposts.[22] The Nigerian columns then went on the defensive, retreating back to Nigerian territory. For this failure, Colonel Carter was replaced by Lieutenant Colonel Frederick Cunliffe, who was placed in command of British operations in northern Cameroon.[23] While the Nigerians invaded Cameroon across the Nigerian border, the French, with support from the Belgian Congo, invaded from French Equatorial Africa and were more successful in their opening engagements.[24]

Brigadier General Charles Dobell, the Canadian Inspector General of the WAFF, was named commander of the Allied expeditionary force to direct joint operations in the Cameroon campaign. The initial objective given to Dobell was the capture of the coastal towns of Victoria, Buea, and Duala. The Colonial Office, however, did not give Dobell instructions to proceed past Duala and conquer the entire colony. The geographic difficulties of numerous swamps and mangroves on the coast ensured that Dobell had to launch a seaborne invasion, rather than a territorial invasion from Calabar in Nigeria, to achieve his initial objectives. Dobell intended that the British and French columns advancing overland across the Cameroonian borders were to coordinate with the Allied attack on Duala. However, poor communication networks and extreme geographical distances largely inhibited this from happening.[25] By 24 September, Dobell's British and French joint expeditionary force of 354 Europeans, 1,859 Africans, and 1,000 carriers positioned itself in transport ships outside Duala, anchored in the Cameroon estuary.[26]

Due to the German defensive positions deeper in Cameroon, the Allied capture of Duala was largely unopposed. Anchored just outside Duala, Dobell sent word to the German governor that he intended to bombard the town unless the Germans surrendered.[27] On the 27th, the Germans destroyed the Duala wireless transmitter and a German lieutenant subsequently surrendered the town with what little military stores they had left. The day before, the last *Schutztruppe* forces at Duala fell back with what they could along the railways into the interior.[28]

Although most of the Gambia Company had remained in the Gambia completing defensive measures and training during this period, a detachment of the company was at Duala at the time of its conquest. On 10 September, the small signaling detachment, led by Lieutenant A. Inglis, embarked on General Dobell's ship, the *Appam*. Bathurst was one of the *Appam's* stops on its voyage from Liverpool to Duala to pick up French and British colonial troops at various West African port towns.[29] The Gambia detachment was to form a signal unit for various columns within Dobell's expeditionary force; however, after arrival at Duala "it was found that the denseness of the forest prevented signaling on any large scale."[30] As a result, Lieutenant Inglis was named as camp commandant of General Dobell's headquarters at Duala, while the rest of the detachment transferred into various units at Duala until they rejoined the main body of the Gambia Company upon its arrival.[31]

With the capture of Duala, the British achieved their initial objectives in Cameroon—the wireless transmitter was destroyed, and the Allies were in possession of Duala's port facilities. However, the British Committee for

Imperial Defense argued that the Germans still had a substantial force spread throughout Cameroon, and in order to secure possession of Duala and remove German pressure on the Nigerian border, General Dobell needed to advance his forces into the interior to defeat the *Schutztruppe* outright. The Colonial Office subsequently informed General Dobell that the new objective in Cameroon was the "complete reduction of the German colony."[32] On 5 October, General Dobell ordered the advance of two columns north from Duala into the interior under the command of Colonel E. Howard Gorges and Lieutenant Colonel A. Haywood, while the French columns continued their advance from the east. By 7 October, the French secured the vital bridge on the Midland Railway which ran towards Edea and eventually Yaunde.[33]

From October to December, General Dobell's forces were successful in advancing north along the Wuri River and Northern Railway, eventually capturing the town of Chang, but the situation east of Duala at Edea had rapidly deteriorated.[34] Although the Allies outnumbered the *Schutztruppe* in the Duala hinterland region, they discovered that coordination between advancing columns was difficult because of poor communication, supply, and transport due to the nature of the geography. The majority of the British contingent was positioned along the Northern Railway, but the French column discovered that a large contingent of *Schutztruppe* fell back along the Midland Railway from Duala and joined an already substantial German force at Edea. Consequently, the French did not take Edea until January, 1915. This general situation forced General Dobell to call for West African Frontier Force reinforcements and give more attention to operations in that area.[35] By this time, General's Dobell's advance out of Duala into the Cameroon interior was significantly bogged down by both substantial German resistance and difficult geography.

On 25 December, Edward Cameron, the Governor of the Gambia, received a telegram from General Dobell requesting another detachment of the Gambia Company, of half company strength, to proceed to Duala immediately.[36] However, the Gambia was not the only colony to provide General Dobell with reinforcements. Four companies of the Sierra Leone Battalion WAFF were also requested to reinforce the Allied contingent in Cameroon.[37]

Captain Thurston, Officer Commanding (OC) of the Gambia Company, with Lieutenant Markham-Rose, 50 rank-and-file, one interpreter, and seven carriers left Bathurst for Duala on 15 January, 1915. The detachment reached Duala on 27 January. At the time of the Gambia Company detachment's arrival in Cameroon, German operations were confusing the British as the Germans routinely avoided large engagements and opted for small skirmishes. On 13 February, a small German force made two unsuccessful attacks on the British forces at the Dibombe Post on the Dibombe River north of Duala. Lieutenant Markham-Rose with six rank-and-file and the Gambia Company's machine gun immediately advanced to the post the same day to reinforce the defenders. Between the 15th and 17th, the British received various intelligence reports that a strong German force of almost 400 men left Yaunde, an increasingly important *Schutztruppe* garrison, and headed towards Yabasi, which was in the vicinity of the Dibombe Post. General Dobell ordered Captain Thurston to reinforce the post with the remaining Gambia Company detachment and one company of the West African Regiment, having arrived there in the afternoon on the 17th. However, new intelligence showed that a large German force was positioned at Ndokama, about 40 kilometers northeast of Duala, and was apparently making an advance on Duala. Only moments after the detachment under Captain Thurston arrived at Dibombe Post, the Gambians were ordered back to Duala as a precaution. They proceeded down the Wuri River on a surf boat, but in the early hours of the 18th, the surf boat capsized. Lance Corporal Momodu Sidibi drowned and some supplies were lost, but the rest of the force was unharmed and eventually returned to Duala. Lance Corporal Sidibi was the first Gambian soldier to lose his life during the war.[38]

Captain Thurston remained at the Dibombe Post in command of the WAR company and the twelve Gambian soldiers still positioned there. Coordinating with the Gold Coast Regiment under Lieutenant Colonel Rose, Captain Thurston advanced towards Ndokama and initially engaged a small *Schutztruppe* detachment of forty soldiers which quickly fled. The Gambian and WAR detachment reached Ndokama on the 22nd with no resistance and found the town evacuated by the Germans. Before they evacuated Ndokama, the Germans intended an advance on Duala based on the mistaken belief that German cruisers captured the Cameroon estuary, but they discovered the truth in time to retreat. Such an incident shows how the *Schutztruppe* in Cameroon was largely functioning "in the dark" without efficient communication with German military authorities in Berlin who could confirm or deny rumors of German naval activity on the coast.[39] Captain Thurston and the rest of the Gambia Company detachment, including the force sent to Duala, returned to Dibombe Post on the 25th.[40]

The Gambia Company remained at Dibombe Post throughout March, only being attacked once on the 11th and sustaining no casualties. However, reports showed that the Germans had reoccupied the town of Yabasi, which was just north of Dibombe Post, with a force of almost 200 soldiers. On the 29th, the Gambia Company joined Lieutenant Colonel Haywood's column which advanced north along the Wuri River towards Yabasi. Under the command of

Captain Thurston, the Gambia Company, one company of the WAR, and fifty rank-and-file from the 2nd Battalion Nigeria Regiment (2 NR) formed the right flank column to Haywood's main column. The right flank column advanced to cut off a road about eight kilometers east of Yabasi while the main column advanced on the town itself. Like Ndokama, the Germans evacuated Yabasi before Haywood's main column arrived, giving up the town without a fight. The Gambia Company subsequently marched back to Dibombe Post and eventually returned to Duala on 1 April.[41]

By April, British strategic objectives in Cameroon changed once again. The growing cost of the campaign made it impossible for the British colonies and Colonial Office to continue footing the bill for operations. Therefore, the War Office took control of all military activities on 3 April; however, General Dobell still received instructions concerning political, civil, and commercial matters from the Colonial Office. As a result, more financial, personnel, and material support was given to the Cameroon campaign from London.[42] Additionally, the German withdrawal from Yabasi, the vicinity around Dibombe Post, and subsequently the rest of the Northern Railway allowed General Dobell to send part of his British contingent to act in conjunction with the French advancing eastward from Edea.[43] Now French and British columns could cooperate effectively in their advance towards Yaunde, where the largest *Schutztruppe* force and the German colonial government were located. This became General Dobell's main objective in Cameroon.[44]

The Gambia Company received its first substantial test in combat on 3 May as part of Haywood's advance towards Yaunde. From Edea, Haywood's column coordinated with a French column and advanced along the Kele River and the Edea-Yaunde road towards Ngwe, securing the town on 12 April. For the rest of April, Haywood's column and the Gambia Company strengthened its position at Ngwe and prepared to continue its advance, which began on 1 May. Two days later, with the Gambia Company as advanced guard, the column came upon the Mbila River near Wum Biagas. The bridge needed to cross the river was destroyed and the Germans were placed in concealed positions and trenches on the opposite bank. The Gambia Company immediately came under fire and scrambled to retaliate. Lieutenant Markham-Rose, who was in command of the company as Captain Thurston remained at Ngwe for base construction duties, was quickly killed by enemy fire.[45] CSM Ebrima Jalu then took command of the company in "one of the hottest parts of the firing line." For his actions, Jalu was awarded the Distinguished Conduct Medal as "he displayed the greatest coolness, and showed a fine example by the way in which he controlled his men and directed their fire throughout the day."[46] Haywood eventually ordered a flanking maneuver to the right of the German positions, which secured the town of Wum Biagas and reduced the German threat against the Gambia Company positions. However, by the end of the day, the Gambia Company sustained four more casualties—Sergeant Momodu Keita and Machine Gunner Ali Kamara were killed, and Privates Abu Bokari and John Cole wounded.[47]

After strengthening the Allied position at Wum Biagas, Haywood resumed his advance towards Yaunde on 25 May. Captain Thurston, having returned to the company, was in command of the right flank column composed of the Gambia Company and one company of 2 NR. The right flank column first attacked an enemy position at a crossroad on the Edea-Yaunde road near Boga. The *Schutztruppe* position was quickly overrun, and the Gambia Company suffered no casualties. The next day, Thurston's force encountered heavy fighting near the village of Ntim where Captain Thurston was wounded and the Gambia Company was subsequently placed under the command of D Company of 2 NR.[48] Until 13 June, the Gambia Company proceeded with Haywood's column along the Edea-Yaunde road, however, the force encountered growing logistical problems and increasing enemy resistance which greatly limited the Allied advance. Soon they were completely bogged down by the Germans and the dense forest environment, only advancing an average of a kilometer and a half per day. The German used the terrain to best advantage, employing highly concealed positions and attacks against the column's flanks. Even worse, the rainy season was set to begin by July. General Dobell subsequently ordered the Allied columns advancing towards Yaunde to return to Wum Biagas. In the weeks to follow, the Allies abandoned Wum Biagas and strengthened their defensive positions around Edea.[49]

General Dobell ultimately halted the Allied advance towards Yaunde because of the dismal state of his troops and the rainy season, that once it began would plague the tropical and coastal areas until November. Hampered by sickness, fatigue and supply problems, the Allies had no choice but to end their offensive.[50] In the Gambia Company alone, out of a total force of 61 officers and men, only 34 were considered "effective" and capable of continuing operations by July 1915.[51]

General Dobell used the delay in activity to recuperate and rebuild his forces. Many British officers and NCOs, including Captain Thurston, were sent to Britain on leave, while the African soldiers garrisoned Duala. Dobell told the War Office that he required an additional 1,000 men as reinforcements to eventually resume his advance on Yaunde. In June, the Nigerians in the north captured Garua, which freed up about a battalion of Nigerians to reinforce Dobell, but he still needed more reinforcements from elsewhere. In August, sections of the West India Regiments from Sierra Leone and the 5th Light Infantry of the Indian Army from Singapore, a force of almost 600 men, landed at Duala, while new British officers and NCOs arrived from Britain.[52] Additionally, the rest of the Gambia Company, which previously remained on defensive duties in the Gambia, arrived from Bathurst in September, bringing the Gambia Company in Cameroon to full company strength for the first time.[53]

While the Gambia Company recuperated at Duala, significant strategic developments occurred that increased the importance of the Allies' upcoming advance on Yaunde. In northern Cameroon, the British forces under the command of General Cunliffe occupied Garua on 10 June and subsequently advanced south towards Ngaundere, occupying that town on 29 June. The occupation of both Garua and Ngaundere ensured Allied control of the northern fringe of the Cameroon plateau and pushed German forces towards Yaunde, even though a small *Schutztruppe* garrison remained at Mora, which was north of Garua. With the fall of these garrisons, the German strategic objective of securing the northern portion of Cameroon was falling apart, and they pushed *Schutztruppe* forces south. Additionally, French forces made significant advances in the south and east by occupying such towns as Lomie and Bitam.

Finally, General Dobell used the greater naval assets supplied by the War Office to strengthen the naval blockade around neutral Spanish Muni (today's Equatorial Guinea) to lessen the amount of supplies funneled to the Germans through the territory.[54] Thus, before the rainy season set in, Dobell sought to position his forces around Yaunde in hope that he would compel the Germans either to fight a pitched battle or surrender.[55]

General Dobell planned his advance on Yaunde from Edea along two lines of attack—the British column under Colonel Gorges advancing along the Edea-Yaunde road and the French column advancing along the Midland Railway. While General Dobell's forces would advance on Yaunde from the west, the French forces approached from the north and northeast. Initially, the Gambia Company was placed under the command of Lieutenant Colonel Haywood within Colonel Gorges' column.[56] On 6 October, Haywood's forces advanced towards Wum Biagas, but left the Gambia Company in Ngwe for garrison duties largely because Captain Thurston had yet to return from recuperation leave in Britain. Captain Thurston returned to the company on 16 October, and by the 25th the company was ordered to cross the Kele River and join Lieutenant Colonel Rose's column at Pookapi advancing on Eseka.

On the 28th, Lieutenant A.E. Coombs and roughly half of the Gambia

Company set out on a patrol to establish communication with the French column west of Eseka. Positioned about 9.5 kilometers west of Eseka, French Commandant Mechet ordered Lieutenant Colonel Rose, located at Song Mandeng, to coordinate an attack on Eseka with Rose and Mechet advancing from opposite sides of the town. However, German forces were positioned at Kwang-le-Bong, directly in the way of Rose's advance on Eseka. On the 29th, the Gambia Company with E Company of 2 NR formed the advanced guard in the attack on Kwang-le-Bong, which housed a *Schutztruppe* detachment of about 120 soldiers and four machine guns. As soon as they entered the village, the Gambia Company received fire from the Germans who quickly retreated south towards French positions after the Gambians and Nigerians returned fire. The company sustained one casualty during the engagement—Private Timah Kamara was killed in action. The next day, the Gambia Company again formed the advance guard on their approach towards Eseka. They arrived at the town to find it had already been captured by the French earlier that day.[57]

For all of November and the early part of December, the Gambia Company largely functioned in a support capacity by escorting convoys of carriers from either Ngwe or Wum Biagas to the main columns advancing on Yaunde. On 11 December, the company again joined Lieutenant Colonel Haywood's main column at Njuge for an assault on the town of Chang Mangas. Up to Chang Mangas, the Allies had to fight through dense jungle which effectively concealed German defensive positions; however, between Chang Mangas and Yaunde, a distance of roughly 40 kilometers, the terrain opened up to "less broken country...in favour of the attackers."[58] Therefore, with the capture of Chang Mangas, the Allies could reorganize for the final assault on Yaunde.[59] On the 12th, the Gambia Company formed the advanced guard of the main column and reached Ndog. Throughout the day, the company continually engaged the enemy who offered relatively weak resistance. However, in the course of the fighting, the Gambia Company sustained ten casualties, including Lieutenant Coombs who was shot through both legs. The Gambia Company subsequently pulled back from its advanced position in Haywood's column, which eventually captured Chang Mangas on the 17th.[60]

Colonel Gorges repositioned his forces into four columns for the final advance on Yaunde, which commenced on 23 December. The Gambia Company was initially placed within Gorges' reserve column, but on the 27th it was moved up with 1 NR and took Unguot without any casualties. Throughout this final advance on Yaunde, the Allies faced only meager resistance from the Germans, eventually taking the town on 1 January 1916, largely because the German forces under Governor Ebermaier fled towards Ebolowa in the direction of neutral

Spanish Muni beginning on Christmas Day. The Gambia Company, as part of Major Cole's column, pursued the Germans towards Ebolowa throughout January; however, the farthest they reached was Lolodorf.[61] The German forces had successfully crossed the border into Spanish Muni starting on 4 February with almost 600 German and 6,000 African soldiers, effectively abandoning German control of Cameroon, with the hope of eventually returning to the colony. The isolated *Schutztruppe* garrison of 155 soldiers at Mora in northern Cameroon held out until 18 February, marking the official end of the Cameroon campaign.[62]

The German retreat to neutral Spanish Muni was expected by the Allies, but certain limitations facilitated an almost clear path from Yaunda to Spanish territory through Ebolowa. Firstly, General Dobell was under the impression that "Ebermaier—a man of strong character and the soul of the German defense—had no intention of trying to leave the country but meant to stand and fight at Yaunde as along as possible."[63] Therefore, General Dobell believed that the main German force at Yaunde would put up a staunch resistance before surrendering and made no significant precautions to block its escape in the immediate surrounding area. Secondly, the Allied pursuit from Yaunde was delayed by the mistaken belief that substantial German forces remained north of Yaunde that threatened their positions. Finally, the Allied pursuit to Ebolowa, and eventually the Spanish border, was hampered by supply and communications difficulties.

The Allied columns could not survive off the land as the Germans destroyed everything in their path, while, in order to catch the Germans, the columns needed to advance faster than their logistics permitted. The Campo and Gabon columns in the south under French command might have had an opportunity to block the German escape, however, operations around Yaunde were given manpower and supply priority which limited the Campo and Gabon columns' ability to effectively close off the border in time, which allowed German forces to escape into Spanish territory.[64]

Although the *Schutztruppe* retreat to Spanish Muni effectively relinquished German control of Cameroon, the continued existence of an armed German force in Spanish territory furthered German political objectives in Africa. The Spanish authorities did not have the power to intern and disarm the *Schutztruppe*, nor could the Allies invade neutral Spanish territory to do so. The Germans remained in Spanish Muni until April 1916 when they moved to the Spanish island of Fernando Po (today's Bioko in Equatorial Guinea), where they were reportedly rearming and training "awaiting the day of German victory in Europe before re-establishing themselves as a major West African power."[65]

The continued existence of an armed German force in West Africa did cause fear among the Allies, especially the French, that hostilities could resume in Cameroon; however, such fears were negligible as the continued British naval blockade around Spanish territory made the reemergence of a substantial *Schutztruppe* force impossible.[66]

When the Germans left Cameroon, political and administrative control of the territory was split between the British and French. Ultimately, the French were granted the lion's share of Cameroon based on the British intention to keep the French out of East Africa. The territory was split arbitrarily, with a section of northern Cameroon being incorporated into Nigeria and the previously ceded French territory being reincorporated into French Equatorial Africa. The remaining territory was split administratively between the British and French under League of Nations mandates, again with the French administering a much larger area. Political violence between Anglophone separatists and a Francophone dominated state in Cameroon today is a consequence of such arbitrary partitions of the territory between 1916 and 1919.[67]

After the end of hostilities, the Gambia Company remained in Cameroon until 23 March 1916. From Lolodorf, they marched to Kribi, on the southern coast, where a transport ship took the company to Duala on 4 March. The Gambia Company with three British officers, three British NCOs, 112 rank-and-file, and four machine gun carriers embarked on the *SS Abosso* for Bathurst and arrived on 4 April. The company suffered roughly twenty combat casualties during its operations, however, many more fell ill due to disease brought on by the arduous tropical environment in which they operated. Although the Gambia Company arrived in stages in Cameroon, detachments of the company were active in the campaign from the capture of Duala in September 1914 to the end of operations in early 1916.[68] As a result, the Gambia was represented in the Cameroon campaign for its entirety. Gambian soldiers participated in some of the most important operations of the campaign, whether it be the initial capture of Duala or the final advance on Yaunde.

Due to its actions in Cameroon, the Gambia Company received much praise and a good reputation among British officers, especially within the command structures of the West African Frontier Force. Captain W. Stanford-Samuel, the next commanding officer of the Gambia Company, wrote that the company emerged from the Cameroon campaign "with such praise and esteem for the work they did" that the company developed a strong *espirit de corps* in its ranks.[69] Such approval was not given to every WAFF unit that fought in Cameroon. For example, the Sierra Leone Battalion and the West African Regiment emerged from the Cameroon campaign with a tarnished reputation for incompetence, especially regarding the performance of the Sierra Leonean soldiers in combat situations.[70]

Despite considerable adversity, the Gambia Company ultimately proved itself as a capable and effective combat unit in Cameroon.

Chapter 7
The Home Front

BEFORE THE ENTIRE GAMBIA COMPANY was eventually sent to Cameroon, the contingent left in the Gambia under Captain Freeman sought to strengthen its reserves to replace the potential casualties it might suffer in that campaign. By April 1915, Captain Freeman and colonial administrators discussed the potential and high likelihood that the rest of the Gambia Company would be called on for service in Cameroon. Therefore, the company needed to increase its strength not only to replace potential casualties, but also to continue its mission of colonial defense in the Gambia. It had been routine since its founding for the Gambia Company to gain new recruits from Sierra Leone. However, as has been discussed, colonial and military officials wanted to step away from recruiting Sierra Leoneans in order to create an all-Gambian force.

During 1915, Captain Freeman noted that he "experienced little difficulty in obtaining recruits" from various districts in the Gambia, "even turning away recruits owing to the Company being at full strength."[71] A total of 27 men were enlisted in the Gambia between September 1914 and March 1915. Captain Freeman's chief problem, however, was supplying and training these new recruits. He had only four spare rifles and limited quantities of supplies and uniforms.

Additionally, there was no ammunition available for training purposes, as all ammunition in the Gambia was set aside for defense. Captain Freeman sought to send his new recruits to Sierra Leone for training and the procurement of much needed supplies, but such plans were never implemented before the last contingent of the Gambia Company left Bathurst for active service in Cameroon.[72] Therefore, a significant portion of the Gambia Company, namely the last detachment to arrive in Cameroon, was both underprepared and undertrained for active service. Yet, the Gambia Company was still successful in its operations, largely owing to the experience gained by the previous contingents initially sent to Cameroon.

The Gambia Company returned from Cameroon on 4 April, 1916. Upon arrival, the governor awarded medals of bravery to various members of the company after a parade through Bathurst's main square. St. Mary's Cathedral offered a Thanksgiving service for the men, and a ball was thrown in the company's honor. However, the British Empire, and by extension the Gambia, was still in a state of war which required the Gambia Company to return to its defensive responsibilities as outlined in the Gambia Defense Scheme. The company took up the same defensive positions that it manned before leaving for Cameroon and continued general training at Cape St. Mary. On 5 May, Captain Thurston left the Gambia for a staff appointment in London and Captain W. Stanford-Samuel, who joined the company in Cameroon, took over command of the Gambia Company.[73]

However, Captain Samuel's command created some discontent with his superiors in the West African Frontier Force. By July, Samuel, who had previously served in France as part of the British Army, initiated new training programs in the company, to include platoon drill based on "double company" organization. The double company system, which reduced the number of companies within an infantry battalion from eight to four essentially doubling the size of a company, was introduced into the British Army in 1913 from lessons learned from the Second Anglo-Boer War (1899-1902) under the view that "a larger company with more subunits was more maneuverable than a smaller one."[74] Not only was the Gambia Company incapable of carrying out platoon tactics based on double company organization since it only had the strength of one company, but such tactics were not yet approved for use within the WAFF. Furthermore, Samuel sought other reforms in training and organization, like marksmanship and Gambian soldiers wearing "chupplies," studded leather sandals, that his WAFF superiors viewed as both impossible and unnecessary to implement.

For instance, chupplies were initially not authorized for use in the Gambia Company as soldiers were often bare foot, even during active service. Some units of the WAFF, especially in Nigeria, were issued chupplies, but such provision never reached the Gambia before the Cameroon and East Africa campaigns. Boots were issued to the Gambia Company, and the rest of the WAFF, for use during the East Africa campaign due to the laborious nature of the campaign and long-distance marches.[75]

Such strong resistance to the introduction of new tactics and procedures in the WAFF illustrates the fact that there was a disconnect between development of the British Army in Europe and the British colonial forces worldwide during the First World War. The British often found it difficult to disseminate lessons learned from the Western Front to other theaters of war and understood that the uniqueness of each theater called for the application of different tactics and procedures that the conditions warranted. Therefore, various forces, to include the WAFF, were given flexibility in their operations and training and "not obliged to adhere to [the] Western Front practices" of the British Army.[76]

Captain Thurston, the previous commander of the Gambia Company, was contacted for his opinion and responded "that Stanford-Samuel is trying to bring too many reforms and unless he is stayed will only puzzle the men and put back their efficiency."[77] In the time that the Gambia Company was supposed to be recovering from the Cameroon campaign and preparing for potential active service in East Africa, Samuel's initiative was not warmly received. Additionally, when plans were forming to send the Gambia Company to German East Africa, doubts arose concerning Samuel's ability to lead a company incombat due to having suffered shell shock in France which, as Captain Thurston noted, clearly affected his service in Cameroon.[78] Samuel's case demonstrates the trend whereby many British officers were sent to the colonies as a means to recover from the trenches in Europe, but many found that service in Africa was just as demanding and hazardous. By 20 October, Captain Samuel was relieved of his command and replaced by Captain R. Law.[79]

While it prepared to defend Bathurst against an unlikely German attack, the Gambia Company was also called upon to defend the colony against a seeming invasion of refugees from French West Africa. In 1912, the French initiated a system of partial conscription in their African colonies with the immediate intention to create a large *Tirailleurs Senegalais* force for its conquest of Morocco, but the system served well for France's long-term goal of the creation of *La Force Noire*. With the onset of war, partial conscription transitioned into virtual universal conscription with annual levies spiking to over 50,000 by 1915.[80] At the time, British West African colonies did not institute a conscription system as recruitment for soldiers in the WAFF, as opposed to carriers, was on a voluntary basis. The recruitment of carriers in British West Africa, however, was often through coercive or forced means, requiring local chiefs to supply certain numbers of people to serve as carriers. Carrier service in British West Africa, and the rest of Africa for that matter, represented a system of forced labor.[81] As a means to avoid conscription and subsequent military service, either in Africa or on the Western Front, many military aged males from French colonial West Africa chose to flee to British territory and avoid mobile draft boards. The Gambia, surrounded almost entirely by French Senegal, turned out to be a convenient and accessible place to avoid French conscription, especially after the conscription spike in 1915.[82]

In December 1916, the Gambia Company was sent to the interior of the colony, eventually reaching the border town of Barokunda, to round up French deserters, but more importantly, as a show of force to dissuade any further illegal migration into the Gambia. Specifically in the area around West Jarra, Fulani people from French territory had crossed the border with their cattle to avoid conscription. There had been reports that such people were living in the bush with their cattle, and even stole sheep, sometimes supported by local Gambians. The Gambia Company, with 200 additional men supplied by a chief, canvassed the area and found the place almost void of deserters. Only five deserters were arrested, while the rest were presumably hiding out in the bush on both sides of the border. The colonial administrator who joined the company on its expedition equated the operation to "manhunting." Although unsuccessful in capturing large numbers of deserters, the operation shows the extent to which migration into the Gambia had become a problem during the First World War, and that the British were willing to use substantial military force to alleviate the situation. In fact, the governor of French West Africa made special appeals to the Gambia colonial government "to assist as far as possible in preventing fugitives from being received into the Protectorate and in dealing with them when found."[83]

Ultimately, the situation was a prominent issue within Anglo-French diplomatic relations. In 1918, when French conscription was ramping up again, one colonial administrator wrote, "as will be remembered the trouble in 1916-1917 became difficult to deal with because rigorous steps were not taken first. The country got full of refugees and eventually a display of military force was necessary."[84] A continuing show of force by the Gambia Company in the border regions was impossible due to its upcoming deployment to German East Africa, therefore, illegal migration into the Gambia would represent an ongoing problem throughout the war that the Gambia Company could do little to lessen.

Discussions to send the Gambia Company on active service to German East Africa began in June 1916 when the company initially "volunteered" for deployment. In a letter dated 16 June, Captain Stanford-Samuel offered the services of the Gambia Company "in East Africa or elsewhere," stating that the majority, but not all, of the rank-and-file and all of the British ranks were willing and desired to "again take up the burden of the Empire" after their recent successes in Cameroon.[85] However, the Gambia Company's true desire and readiness to volunteer for service in East Africa appears to have been invented by Captain Stanford-Samuel. Having returned to the Gambia only two months prior, the Gambia Company was in no state to quickly return to active service. At the time, only 60 to 70 percent of the company was considered fit for operations, and as Captain Thurston explained after his departure from the Gambia, he discharged a good number of soldiers who failed to perform well in Cameroon and their replacements were not yet efficiently trained. Furthermore, Thurston stated that "a lot of the men were very tired of active service before the end of the Cameroons [*sic*] operations."[86] Surely, in the span of only two months the Gambia Company was not able, nor was the entire company willing, to jump back into active service in East Africa. In August, Colonial Secretary Bonar Law viewed the Gambia Company's offer of active service both unnecessary and inadvisable, as he preferred for the company to remain in the Gambia for defense and continued training.[87] By this time, the only West African Frontier Force unit in German East Africa was the Gold Coast Regiment.[88]

In December 1916 the situation changed for the Gambia Company when the British were in the process of "Africanizing" the East Africa campaign. Initially, British forces in East Africa consisted largely of Indian, white South African, and some British soldiers due to the lack of substantial locally recruited colonial militaries in the region. White settler fears of potential armed rebellions of Africans limited the prewar development of such colonial militaries as the King's African Rifles (KAR) in eastern and southern Africa. However, the British, Indian, and white South African soldiers were vulnerable to tropical disease, like malaria and dysentery, that ravaged German East Africa and extremely large numbers became invalid in only a couple months of service. By the end of 1916, almost 12,000 South Africans were forced home due to illness, exhaustion, and other factors—in one case a South African battalion was just 10 percent effective. The British believed that African soldiers were more resistant to tropical diseases, but also, the British needed additional manpower to replace the invalid soldiers. Therefore, the British sought to Africanize the East African campaign by greatly expanding the KAR and deploying the WAFF. Since KAR expansion would take time, the WAFF was ordered to deploy immediately to East Africa. The Nigerian Brigade joined the GCR, which was present in East Africa since July 1916, in December.[89] On 8 December, Secretary Bonar Law requested that the Gambia Company accompany the Nigerian contingent in East Africa.[90] This was based on the company's previous commitment of active service months prior, but also on the reputation that the company had been an effective unit during the Cameroon campaign.[91]

However, the Gambia Company was not yet prepared for active service or able to leave its defensive responsibilities without some sort of replacement. The company was short on British officers, without proper supplies and weaponry, still needed to complete training, and had to enlist the carriers that were required for the campaign. The War Office required that 275 carriers accompany the Gambia Company to East Africa, owing to the extreme logistical demands of the East African Campaign. However, Captain R. Law, commanding officer of the Gambia Company, found that enlisting carriers in the Gambia was nearly impossible without conscription due to the colony's size and the unwillingness of chiefs to give up so many men. Therefore, the governor of Sierra Leone agreed that the required carriers could be enlisted from his colony, while additional British officers could be taken from the Sierra Leone Battalion. It must be noted that both the SLB and the West African Regiment were not considered for active service in German East Africa due to British arguments that they performed poorly during the Cameroon campaign. Rather, due to the perception of Sierra Leoneans having an "unwarlike character," contrary to the previous view of the Mende and Temne having "martial" qualities, large numbers of carriers were recruited for the Sierra Leone Carrier Corps and sent to East Africa to serve in non-combat roles.[92] H Company of the WAR stationed in Sierra Leone arrived in Bathurst in March 1917 to take over the Gambia Company's defensive responsibilities.[93] With such things in order, the Gambia Company embarked on 13 April for service in German East Africa.[94]

After the Gambia Company departed, there was considerable effort within the Gambia itself to enlist a reserve force in anticipation of heavy casualties and the eventual need for reinforcement. By the time of the company's departure, the onerous and wasteful nature of operations in East Africa was well known. This forced Captain Law to argue that "We shall have casualties, and unless an effort is made to keep us reinforced, we shall be filled up with other troops, and eventually the Gambia 'Company' would cease to exist."[95] Authorities assumed that the Gambia Company would sustain casualties at a rate of thirty per month. Therefore, one British NCO and four experienced Gambian soldiers were left in the colony to help raise and train a reserve force at Cape St. Mary and a newly established training center to be constructed within Bathurst. It was believed that an initial reserve force of 250 volunteers could be easily obtained, however, recruiting was limited by more lucrative labor opportunities in the colony. Recruitment in the Gambia, and the rest of British West Africa, was always contingent upon labor demands. Since the British never imposed strict conscription laws like the French, many potential recruits preferred to seek better paying and safer jobs in the civilian economy. However, West African Frontier Force recruiters found that individuals were more willing to enlist during the dry season when work was not as readily available.[96]

By May, Captains Leese and Greig, Sierra Leone Battalion officers who were temporarily attached to the company, took over recruiting and were only successful in enlisting fifty men. Governor Cameron argued that "As things are now I doubt [*sic*] extremely if we can ever expect to get the 250 men laid out for by Colonel Haywood [director of recruiting for the WAFF] without resorting to a measure of compulsion."[97] By July, the number of recruits only rose to 118, while training was limited due to the fact that there were not enough rifles and other supplies. Eventually, Governor Cameron sent a notice out to all chiefs requiring each of them to produce at least 25 men for service as reserves for the Gambia Company, while the War Office ordered that the initial batch of recruits in the Gambia be sent to East Africa untrained as training would be completed once they arrived. Although not an official form of conscription, Governor Cameron's letter to the chiefs resembled a form of recruitment by compulsion and showed the extent that British officials were desperate to fulfill manpower needs in East Africa and ensure the continued existence of the Gambia Company as an entity.[98] Fortunately, such coercive recruitment would not last long nor would substantial numbers of Gambian reinforcements be sent to German East Africa due to the drawdown of WAFF involvement and the continued expansion of the King's African Rifles in the campaign beginning in October 1917. By the end of the campaign, only 100 Gambians were sent to East Africa as reinforcements, none of whom saw combat.[99]

As the officer in charge of recruiting in West Africa, Colonel Haywood had even grander views of the potential supply of manpower for the WAFF and asked Captain Law to develop a report on the absolute greatest number of men that the Gambia could supply for military service, either as soldiers or carriers. Part of this inquiry stemmed from not knowing how long hostilities would continue in German East Africa and elsewhere, while it was also perceived that the Gambia was not contributing enough to the war effort compared to the other colonies. Captain Law concluded that only through compulsory recruitment could the Gambia raise about 2,000 men for service in East Africa or elsewhere, should it be needed. Such a figure did not sit well with Governor Cameron who emphasized the Gambia's uniqueness in size and very limited resources compared to the rest of British West Africa. He contested that "It does not seem to me exactly worthwhile from the point of view of the Imperial Government, to exploit a small narrow strip of country like this for numerical results which are unlikely to be commensurate with the contingent trouble and expense, when there are so many wider fields to draw from."[100] The Gambia surely could not supply the same amount of military resources and manpower as its sister colonies, as even the creation of a reserve force of 250 men was nearly impossible.

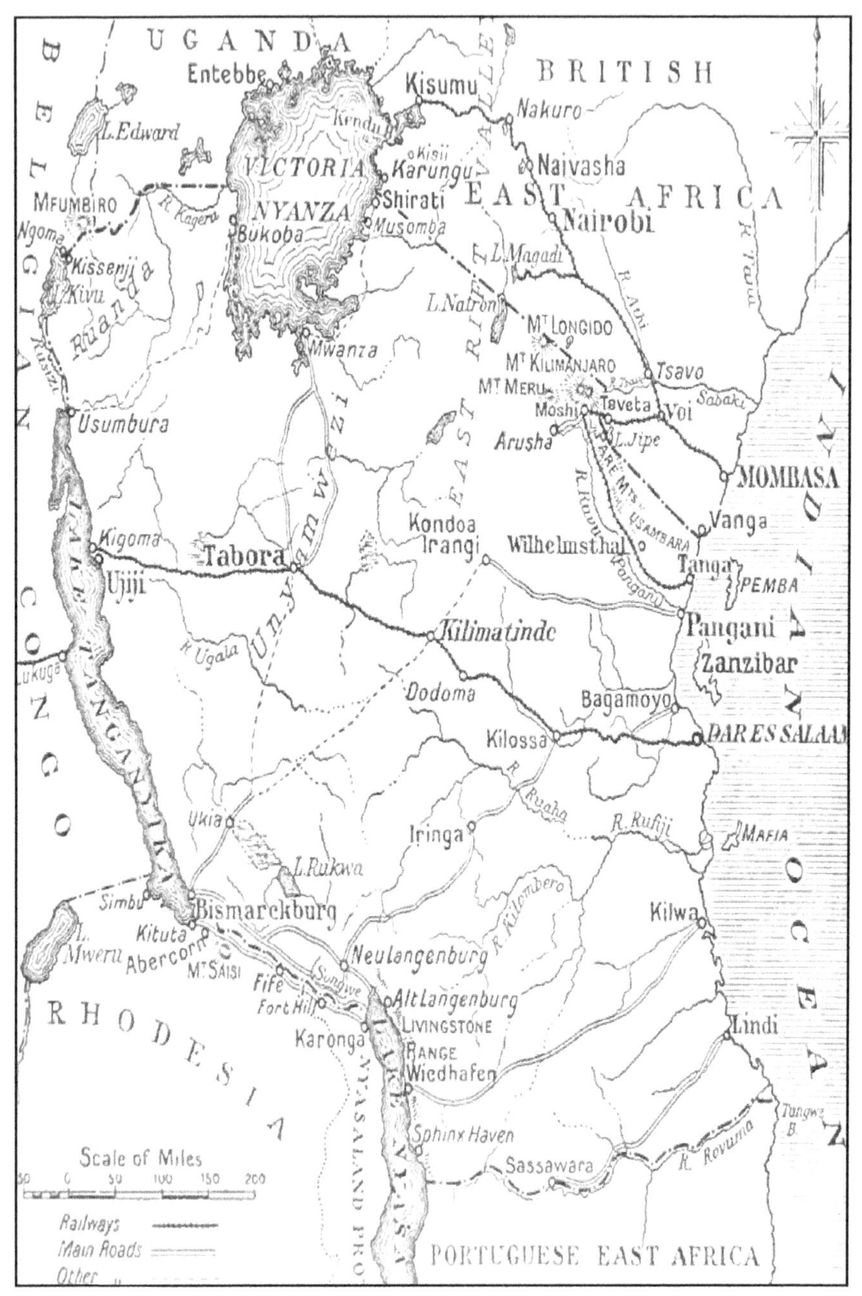
UGANDA
BRITISH
EAST AFRICA
BELGIAN CONGO
RHODESIA
PORTUGUESE EAST AFRICA
INDIAN OCEAN
VICTORIA NYANZA
LAKE TANGANYIKA
Entebbe
Kisumu
Nakuro
Naivasha
Nairobi
Kendu
Kisii
Karungu
Shirati
Musomba
Bukoba
L. Edward
MFUMBIRO
R. Kagera
Ngoma
Kissenji
L. Kivu
Ruanda
Rusizi
Usumbura
Mwanza
L. Magadi
L. Natron
MT LONGIDO
MT KILIMANJARO
MT MERU
Moshi
Taveta
Tsavo
Voi
Sabaki
R. Tana
R. Athi
L. Jipe
Arusha
MOMBASA
Vanga
PARE MTS
USAMBARA
Wilhelmsthal
R. Pangani
Tanga
PEMBA
Pangani
Zanzibar
Kondoa Irangi
Tabora
Kigoma
Ujiji
Unyamwezi
EAST RIFT VALLEY
Kilimatinde
R. Ugala
Lukuga
Dodoma
Bagamoyo
Kilossa
DAR ES SALAAM
R. Ruaha
R. Rufiji
MAFIA
Iringa
Ukia
L. Rukwa
Simbu
Bismarckburg
R. Kilombero
Kilwa
L. Mweru
Kituta
Abercorn
MT SAISI
Fife
Songwe
Neulangenburg
Fort Hill
Alt Langenburg
LIVINGSTONE RANGE
Karonga
Lindi
Wiedhafen
LAKE NYASA
NYASALAND PRO
Sphinx Haven
Sassawara
R. Rovuma
Tungwe B.
Scale of Miles
50 0 50 100 150 200
Railways
Main Roads
Other

Chapter 8
Operations in German East Africa

MUCH LIKE THEIR STRATEGY IN CAMEROON, the Germans sought to maintain some sort of claim to German East Africa during the war so that upon anticipated peace negotiations they could retain their position as an imperial power in Africa. With the onset of war, Heinrich Schnee, governor of German East Africa, decided to follow a plan developed by the Germans before the war, "to abandon the coast and withdraw inland to where the British could not easily follow."[101] However, Lieutenant Colonel Paul von Lettow Vorbeck, commander of the *Schutztruppe* in German East Africa, despised such a plan "because of its connotations of cowardice," even though it eventually benefitted his strategic objectives.[102] In effect, Lettow consolidated *Schutztruppe* forces in the interior of the territory and the last German naval asset in the region, the *Konigsberg*, distracted British naval authorities. Again, the German strategy supported the initial British objective in German East Africa, which was to secure keys ports and naval facilities on the coast. However, as the campaign developed, the British objective changed "to bring the whole of German East Africa under British authority."[103]

By 1914, the British colonial military in British East Africa (today's Kenya), the King's African Rifles,was not prepared for a substantial military campaign against the *Schutztruppe*. Recently the KAR had been reduced by a whole battalion out of white settler fears of arming Africans. Additionally, the KAR had the responsibility for protecting British East Africa and its valuable railways against German attacks. Therefore, the British ordered the Indian Army to send Indian Expeditionary Forces (IEF), IEF B and IEF C, to East Africa and help capture valuable German ports on the coast. Other lettered Indian Expeditionary Forces were sent to various fronts, like IEF A to the Western Front. The East Africa campaign ultimately started on 2 November 1914 when IEF C invaded German territory from Kenya. IEF C's overland invasion was to help support IEF B's amphibious invasion at the port town of Tanga; however, a large *Schutztruppe* force under Lettow pushed IEF C back and subsequently reinforced the German garrison at Tanga by train to help drive back IEF B as well. Tanga was a disaster for the British.[104] As a result, British control of the campaign soon shifted from the India and Colonial Offices to the War Office, while victory at Tanga allowed Lettow to wrestle greater operational control away from Schnee and gain time to prepare for future British offensives.[105] The Battle of Tanga initiated what would become a drawn out and devastating campaign in German East Africa.

Lettow's military strategy in German East Africa was ultimately one of survival to drain Allied military resources away from the European theater and ensure continued German possession of territory in Africa. Initially, he sought a decisive battle against the British. The Battle of Tanga gave Lettow the opportunity for a decisive engagement, but it showed the *Schutztruppe*'s severe disadvantage in terms of manpower and logistics. German East Africa was essentially surrounded on all sides by Allied, or soon to be Allied, colonial powers.

Furthermore, the British Navy controlled the coast, which inhibited further resupply and reinforcements for the *Schutztruppe*. Therefore, the Germans would have to calculate the impact of any large-scale engagement to ensure the *Schutztruppe* could remain as a force in being, while the British could be resupplied at will with manpower and materiel through their command of the sea. After the victory at Tanga, from which he secured large amounts of weapons and equipment left by the retreating IEFs, Lettow shifted his strategy to an operational approach centered on *Schutztruppe* survival. He increased his force by recruiting soldiers and conscripting carriers from the local population, while capturing, and subsequently rationing, supplies from his enemies. Additionally, Lettow seized food from local communities. The vast size of German East Africa and the lack of substantial transportation infrastructure facilitated Lettow's elusiveness throughout the campaign. German East Africa had one major railway, the Central Railway, that ran from Dar es Salaam to Lake Tanganyika. The Usambara Railway in the north and the Rufigi River were also important transportation lines, but other than that, German East Africa lacked substantial infrastructure development before 1914.[106] However, this did not limit Lettow from taking to the offensive and subsequently retiring after engagements to preserve his force for as long as possible. He believed in a protracted resistance where "the *Schutztruppe* would draw British troops away from the main theatre and employ British warships in oceanic escort duties from home waters."[107] In effect, Lettow contributed to the war in Europe by waging a costly war in German East Africa—the longer he could carry out his resistance, the greater benefit he would give to the Germans on the Western Front. In reality, the British forces sent to German East Africa, except possibly the South Africans, were never destined for the Western Front due to British racial conceptions of their colonial soldiers. Even still, Lettow was somewhat successful in diverting precious military materiel away from Europe.[108]

Lettow's strategic outlook translated into sustained combat operations throughout almost the entirety of German East Africa and surrounding territories. In 1915, he focused his efforts on the defense of the western portions of the territory: "the wheat production of the Neu Langenburg area, the head of the central railway at Kigoma, and the navigation of Lake Tanganyika."[109] Additionally, the *Schutztruppe* continually raided specific targets in Belgian and British territory, to include the Uganda Railway, to both gather supplies and disrupt Allied advances against German positions. However, in 1916 circumstances grew more difficult for the *Schutztruppe*. The campaign in German South West Africa had recently concluded, which freed up roughly 13,000 South African troops for service in German East Africa. Additionally, the Portuguese were sending more troops for the defense of their African territory and the eventual invasion of German East Africa. As a result, the Allies prepared an invasion of German East Africa across three lines of advance.[110] In March 1916, under the command of South African Lieutenant General Jan Christian Smuts, the British invaded from Kenya through the Kilimanjaro area, while other invasions commenced from the Belgian Congo, Northern Rhodesia, and Nyasaland in the west and southwest.[111]

By September, the British had secured German territory up to the Central Railway and Dar es Salaam, effectively cornering the *Schutztruppe* in the southeastern portion of German East Africa. However, with the onset of the rainy season, Smuts was forced to halt the Allied advance until December when the Nigerian Brigade arrived. Meanwhile, the British were busy building up the King's African Rifles in an attempt, with the addition of the West African Frontier Force, to fully Africanize the East Africa campaign.[112] In the first half of 1917, the British only made minor advances against the *Schutztruppe*, while KAR commander General Arthur Hoskins took over command of the Allied forces. Hoskins effectively rebuilt and reorganized the Allied forces between February and May, which gave his successor, South African General Jacob van Deventer, a substantial force capable of pushing the *Schutztruppe* out of German East Africa in the following months.[113]

The Gambia Company, under the command of Captain Law, left Bathurst on 15 April, 1917 aboard the *HMT City of Sparta* with one other British officer, one British NCO, 127 rank- and-file, eight machine gun carriers, and 75 other carriers. After two days, the company arrived in Freetown, where it disembarked and made camp at Murray Town until 16 May. During its time in Sierra Leone, the Gambia Company continuously trained for its upcoming combat operations with its new Lewis Guns.[114] Lewis Guns were light machine guns which were more mobile than larger machine guns like the Maxim. In fact, the Gambia Company was the first WAFF unit to be supplied with Lewis Guns. They also used the time in Sierra Leone to procure an additional 200 carriers for service in East Africa.[115] The carriers attached to the Gambia Company were recruited from the area immediately surrounding the town of Songo, about 50 kilometers outside of Freetown, by Captain Law and his lieutenants. In addition to the 200 carriers, three British officers (Lieutenants Reed, Spens, and Devlin) joined the company from the Sierra Leone Battalion. Aboard the *City of Sparta*, with the Sierra Leonean carriers on another ship, the company left Freetown on 20 May and finally arrived at the occupied German East Africa port of Dar es Salaam on 20 June with brief stops at Cape Town and Durban.[116]

The Gambia Company remained at Dar es Salaam until 30 June when it travelled to Morogoro, about 185 kilometers west of Dar es Salaam, by train. In the meantime, Captain Law learned that the Sierra Leonean carriers had landed and were immediately sent to the Labour Battalion camp under the control of the Military Labour Bureau (MLB) to join the West African Carrier Corps. This situation shows the massive demand for carriers during the East Africa campaign. Both sides used carriers as logistical support for advancing columns, and exploited this form of labor, considering it the best suited for use in the demanding operational environments of Africa. The British alone utilized about one million carriers in the East African Campaign to support combat operations, with nearly 100,000 dying from disease and exhaustion.[117]

Upon hearing the news of the loss of most of their carriers to the MLB, Captain Law sent a letter of protest, but to no avail. The carrier contingent was subsequently sent out for immediate service, while the officer in charge of the contingent, Lieutenant Reed, did not rejoin the Gambia Company until 2 September. Eventually, only 126 of the original 200 Sierra Leonean carriers rejoined the company on 3 October. With only the original 75 carriers from the Gambia, the Gambia Company completed general training near Morogoro at Greitz Farm until 14 August when it returned to Dar es Salaam.[118] While there, the Gambia Company was issued new equipment, including boots, in anticipation of the long and laborious marches to come. They also continued to train. Captain Law noted, "Acting upon the experience gained by the Nigerian Brigade with regard to the necessity of foot protection for the troops, owing to the rough and thorny nature of the country I decided to equip the Company as far as possible with boots, in preference to Sandals or Chupplies." This is significant, because in the past, WAFF units and the Gambia Company usually went into combat barefoot.[119]

Captain Law observed that due to its time at Greitz Farm, the Gambia Company had shown much improvement in terms of training and were ready for "active service conditions."[120] However, training only provided a glimpse of the realities of active operations in German East Africa and the conditions the company would face. In a little more than a month, the Gambia Company had sustained numerous hospitalizations and a couple of deaths due to illness. Captain Law noted that "there have been several cases of pneumonia among the company, owing to the change of climate."[121] High rates of illness among soldiers and carriers was characteristic of operations in East Africa, which represented a main reason why the WAFF was called on to replace the South Africans in 1916. Although the West African units still suffered from illness, they fared better than the South Africans and remained effective combat formations.[122]

By August 1917, General van Deventer was preparing for his final advance south against the *Schutztruppe*. In cooperation with Norforce, the British column from Northern Rhodesia/Nyasaland under Lieutenant Colonel Edward Northey, and the Belgians to the west, van Deventer positioned his forces, Hanforce and Linforce, at Kilwa and Lindi respectively.

General van Deventer believed that Lettow might cross into Portuguese territory (today's Mozambique), so he arranged the Allied advance to cut off the *Schutztruppe* retreat south. Hanforce would push the *Schutztruppe* south, while Norforce and Linforce would advance from the west and east respectively. The Nigerian Brigade was initially part of Hanforce, but advanced ahead of the main column in late September and early October to support Linforce in its advance along the Lukuledi River towards Nyangao.[123]

Leaving Dar es Salaam on 20 August, the Gambia Company arrived at Kilwa Kisiwani two days later. From there, the company marched roughly 16 kilometers to a camp called Red Hill near Kilwa Kivinje. The company completed more training at Red Hill, to include defending against a mock attack from the 55th Cooks Rifles of the Indian Army, while it waited for the arrival of newly recruited carriers. Finally, on 23 September, the Gambia Company set off to join the Nigerian Brigade, which, the day earlier, had been engaged in a heated battle at Bweho-Chini. From Red Hill, the Gambia Company marched southwest in the direction of Nahungo, while escorting almost 500 carriers, Nigerian reinforcements, and an ambulance company. During the march, the Nigerian Brigade was ordered to join Brigadier General O'Grady's column, part of Linforce, in an attack on substantial German positions at Nyangao. On 2 October, the company linked up with the Nigerian Brigade positioned at Nahungo under the command of Colonel D. Mann, and set off in the direction of Nyangao two days later.[124]

After over a week of marching south to eventually link up with Linforce, the Gambia Company arrived at Namupa Mission on the afternoon of 14 October and received orders for its operations for the next day. The company arrived just in time to participate in one of the most intense engagements of the campaign—the Battle of Mahiwa (Battle of Nyangao). The Gambia Company, with three companies of 1 NR and a section of artillery, were ordered to a position 500 meters west of Nyangao behind the German line to block the Namupa-Nyangao road, which the Germans might use to retreat. The Gambians were in position by 1000 hours after only a short engagement with the enemy. For the rest of the day, company patrols were constantly "in touch" with the Germans.

On the 16th, the Gambia Company and 1 NR were ordered to rejoin the main column at Mahiwa, however, before it could reach the main column, the force came under heavy fire from Mremba Hill.[125] Unknown to the Nigerians, Lettow reinforced Mremba Hill the night before with five companies and two mountain guns under his personal command. At about 1400 hours, German Captain V. Goering with two companies from Lettow's force attacked the Gambia Company and 1 NR when they were south of Namupa Mission between two streams. Major Roberts, commander of 1 NR, ordered that the Gambia Company split into two sections protecting each flank of the main force.[126] Soon, German fire increased and was followed by a "vigorous" attack on the Gambian positions on the right flank. After their attack on the right, the Germans shifted their assault to the Gambian positions on the left flank with three separate advances. The Germans came within 30 meters of Gambian positions during this engagement, while the Gambians exhausted almost all of their ammunition. At about 1630 hours, Colonel Mann ordered the retreat of the force north towards Namupa Mission, with the left half of the Gambia Company covering the retreat after receiving more ammunition.[127] By that night, the Gambia Company and 1 NR returned to Namupa Mission and occupied the trenches protecting the site, while the Germans retired and captured the Gambia Company's supplies which were left behind, to include roughly 150,000 rounds of ammunition.[128]

The engagement in the vicinity of Namupa Mission was significant because it blocked the complete destruction of the Nigerian Brigade. Captain Law noted:

> *It became known some time later that the Gambia Company with three Companies of the 1st Nigeria Regiment, had met Von Lettow himself in command of nine German Companies, who were on their way to 'mop up' the remainder of the Brigade who had become surrounded.*[129]

However, the action on 16 October devastated the Gambia Company. In just one day, fifteen members of the company were killed, including CSM Ebrima Jalu who had been decorated for his actions in the Cameroon Campaign, while another thirteen were wounded. These losses were so devastating to the company because they were largely among NCOs and other soldiers who had fought in Cameroon and so provided valuable experience for the company. Captain Law noted that "the behavior of the men throughout the action left nothing to be desired. The losses among Native NCOs and old soldiers who would have made NCOs will be much felt in the future, they being impossible to replace in this unit."[130]

3 NR was sent to Namupa Mission to reinforce and escort the Gambia Company and 1 NR back to Nyangao, which the Germans had evacuated the day before. On the 18th, the company, again with 1 NR, was ordered to support an attack on a German position on a ridge 3 kilometers southwest of Nyangao. At 1230 hours, the Gambia Company arrived in support of the attack, and segments of the German positions were taken by 1300. Thirty minutes later, the Gambia Company with 1 NR advanced and took over the front line, relieving 3 NR and 2nd KAR. The Gambia Company remained on the front line under continuous fire from German positions, even as the company's machine gun and one Lewis gun were forced out of action. At 1830, the Germans launched a determined attack against the Gambia Company's front, advancing to within 30 meters of the Gambian line. Eventually, the attack was beaten off, and the Germans withdrew for good.[131] After the German withdrawal, the whole British force retired to Nyangao, with the Gambia Company arriving in the town just after midnight.[132] The 18th was another costly day for the Gambia Company. It suffered one killed, Private Modi Jalla, and an additional fifteen wounded. In the span of two days, almost 50 percent of the Gambia Company was either killed or wounded in action.[133]

The Battle of Mahiwa was a costly endeavor for both the British and German forces. Historian Ross Anderson called it "the bloodiest battle of the campaign," as the British lost nearly 40 percent of their strength to casualties and the Germans nearly 30 percent, while both sides expended far more ammunition than they could afford.[134] In the end, neither side achieved a tactical victory. Lettow had the chance to defeat the British in the decisive battle he sought throughout the majority of the campaign, but could not be drawn into an attritional style of warfare that the British were sure to win.

Additionally, at Mahiwa, General van Deventer had the opportunity to deliver a decisive blow to Lettow in hopes of forcing a surrender, but the costly engagement brought van Deventer's advance to a halt in order to recuperate and resupply for further action. This delay effectively gave Lettow a three-week-headstart in his final push to Portuguese territory. By the end of November 1917, all of German East Africa was clear of the *Schutztruppe* as Lettow crossed into Mozambique and pillaged the territory to maintain his force. The Battle of Mahiwa was the last large-scale engagement of the campaign, as Lettow subsequently reduced his force to only the best soldiers and essential personnel to continue his strategy of survival. The battle effectively diminished any hopes of continued *Schutztruppe* presence in German East Africa. Lettow continued this strategy in non-German territory for almost another year, to include minor engagements against Portuguese and KAR forces, until he surrendered to British forces two weeks after the armistice on 25 November 1918 in Northern Rhodesia (today's Zambia), marking the end of the East Africa campaign. In effect, the East Africa campaign was the longest campaign of the First World War.[135]

The action in and around Nyangao was the last substantial combat that the Gambia Company saw in the East Africa campaign. Between 19 October and 5 November, the company remained in Nyangao refitting and performing various patrols, only to have its ranks continually diminished due to illness and injury. By 30 October, only seven British officers and NCOs and fifty-one Gambian rank-and-file were fit for active operations, with the rest of the company either sick or in the hospital recovering from wounds. To add to the Gambia Company's hardships, almost all of its supplies, to include everything from ammunition to cooking pots, were lost during the action on 16 October.[136] On 5 November, the Gambia Company set out from Nyangao to serve as an escort "to the various telephone lines which would be required from the Linforce Advanced Signal Company."[137] Supporting the Allied pursuit of the *Schutztruppe* heading towards Portuguese territory, the Gambia Company was continuously split into small parties to catch up with the speed of the advance. Eventually, the Nigerian Brigade, and by extension the Gambia Company, reached Mtama, about 80 kilometers west of Lindi, on 18 January 1918. At Mtama, the Nigerian Brigade halted its advanced, and on 28 January, received orders to return to West Africa.[138]

The first detachment of the Gambia Company reserve did not join the company until 13 January during its final push towards Mtama. Under the command of Lieutenant O.W. Warren, the detachment of 50 men arrived in East Africa on 15 November 1917, but did not begin its march from Lindi to meet up with the Gambia Company until 9 December. Nonetheless, the arrival of the reserves apparently provided a great morale boost for the rest of the men of the company. Another reserve detachment of 50 men from the Gambia arrived at Dar-es-Salaam on 26 January, but was unable to join the company before its return to West Africa. None of the reserves saw combat in East Africa.[139]

In the course of one battle, the Gambia Company was essentially put out of commission. However, such circumstances were not unique to the Gambians. The Battle of Mahiwa was also the last time the Nigerian Brigade saw substantial combat in East Africa, largely because the development of the King's African Rifles lessened the need for the force, and also because of its decrepit state. After the battle, General van Deventer reorganized his forces in German East Africa by transitioning almost solely to the newly raised KAR battalions, while repatriating other units. The Nigerian Brigade, and by extension the Gambia Company, stayed in East Africa recuperating until February 1918 when it departed out of Lindi.[140] Eventually, the Gambia Company returned to Bathurst on 8 April.[141]

Like Cameroon, German East Africa was subsequently split up among the Allied power under League of Nations mandates. Rwanda and Burundi transferred to Belgian control, southern parts of the territory were absorbed by Portuguese controlled Mozambique, and the rest formed British controlled Tanganyika (the mainland part of today's Tanzania). Following its service in German East Africa, the West African Frontier Force, including the Gambia Company, were prepared for continued active service in the Middle East, but the war concluded before such plans were implemented.[142]

The Gambia Company's experience in the East Africa campaign begs the question as to why the Gambia colonial government, and the British government for that matter, would supply the resources to send one infantry company across the entire continent, when in the end, it only participated in three days of actual combat. In the eyes of some, the Gambia Company was taking up "the burden of the Empire by offering themselves for service in East Africa."[143] No matter the extent of the company's contribution to the East Africa campaign, as long as it supported British strategic interests in Africa it was fulfilling its "imperial duty." Of course, no one in the War Office or Colonial Office could know that as a result of one engagement with the *Schutztruppe* and continuous service in a hazardous and laborious environment that the strength of the Gambia Company would be reduced by half. Nor could they know that the Gambia Company would arrive just in time to fight in one of the heaviest engagements of the campaign. The case proves that as a small independent unit within the WAFF, the Gambia Company could only last in the field for so long before it would eventually dissolve due to combat casualties or disease, especially since it lacked any substantial reserve component.

Overall, the Gambia Company's experience in German East Africa is a testament to the grueling conditions and devastation caused by the campaign. The mobile nature of the campaign put laborious demands on both soldiers and carriers, who operated in a harsh, disease-ridden environment. The British had the luxury, to an extent, of cycling units in and out of the campaign, while German strength gradually diminished with every engagement. The hardship was even greater for the inhabitants of German East Africa, who were either forced into service as carriers and sometimes soldiers on both sides of the conflict or left to live in a land devastated by warfare. Drought combined with British and German efforts to strip the local populations of "men, cattle, and food" left parts of Tanzania with a disastrous famine.[144] Although brief, the Gambia Company's experience gives insight into the demanding nature of warfare in East Africa.

Section Two Conclusion

ANALYZING THE EXPERIENCES of the Gambia Company in the First World War provides a unique perspective on the conflict in Africa. It confirms historian Hew Strachan's argument that "The war in Africa was an affair not of 'big battalions' but of individual companies."[145] The Gambia Company, as the smallest independent unit in the West African Frontier Force, effectively supported and provided a substantial benefit to Allied operations in both the Cameroon and East Africa campaigns. Whether at Yaunde or Nyangao, the company's combat record against the *Schutztruppe* shows that it contributed significantly to Allied successes at crucial moments in both campaigns. The nature of warfare in Africa, which was highly mobile and largely consistent of small-scale engagements, allowed the Gambia Company a significant place in the history of the First World War in Africa despite its smallness and independence within the greater WAFF. However, most importantly, the experiences of both the Gambia Company and the colony it served demonstrate that the First World War truly was a global conflict, affecting even the smallest of territories in a seemingly forgotten part of the world.

Section Three

The Gambia Company during the Interwar Period, 1918-1939

FROM ITS EXPLOITS DURING THE FIRST WORLD WAR, the Gambia Company earned a strong and favorable reputation as an effective military unit within the West African Frontier Force. However, the strains of war quickly caught up with the Gambia Company in the years immediately following the First World War, which significantly hurt its ability to maintain such a favorable reputation. The Gambia Company was forced to deal with personnel, training, and discipline deficiencies which were heightened based on its organization as a relatively small and independent military unit. In effect, continued problems posed by the burden of its institutional independence ensured that the Gambia Company's attachment to a larger WAFF organization was inevitable and facilitated by the Gambia's strategic insignificance within West Africa.

The Gambia Company struggled as a small independent military organization during the interwar era because of various policies and decisions made by British officials following the First World War. For the better part of the period, the Gambia Company routinely lacked military efficiency and was often considered unfit for active service, unlike from its status before the war. However, it is clear that the Gambia Company's eventual attachment to the Sierra Leone Battalion was inevitable whether the Gambia Company was militarily proficient or not. Ultimately, with the Second World War just over the horizon, British officials viewed the military needs of the Gambia as subordinate to that of strategically more important colonial possessions elsewhere in West Africa.

Chapter 9 - Postwar Difficulties

FOLLOWING THE FIRST WORLD WAR, the British Government drastically reduced the size of its military organizations and spending based on the premise of the "Ten Year Rule." The policy stipulated that the First World War had been so destructive that there was no need to equip and maintain a large military, as another war in Europe would not occur for at least another decade. As a result, the British Army drastically reduced in size, but procured more modern armaments. Ultimately, British military officials believed that a "relatively small but highly professional army, equipped with the most modern weapons" would be enough to avoid the stalemate experienced on the Western Front should another war arise.[1]

British military reductions had an even greater effect on the colonial militaries throughout the British Empire, which were decreased in size but did not receive more modern armaments until just before the Second World War. The West African Frontier Force was downsized, in some cases to levels lower than what existed before the war, while the West India Regiments and the West African Regiment were disbanded in 1927 and 1928 respectively.[2] With such military forces no longer stationed in West Africa, the WAFF was forced to take on increased colonial defense obligations with no increase in available resources. The British, however, did introduce airpower across their overseas territories as an effective and cheaper means of colonial policing and control.[3] Additionally, the global economic depression of the 1930s placed further strains on the WAFF through more force reductions and subsequent reorganization.[4]

Beyond the British military situation, the very nature of British imperialism in West Africa and elsewhere changed during the interwar period as a result of the global economic climate. The period was what some historians term "the high tide of colonial rule," where European powers saw their empires as vital to postwar recovery and economic survival in the poor international economic climate of the interwar period.[5] The British wanted to extract as much wealth as possible from their various colonies through stricter control of labor and ensuring African dependence on the wage economy. In response, Africans sought to counter continued social and economic injustices through the creation of workers' unions and welfare associations. In most places, African resistance to European colonialism changed from rebellions, as seen during the conquest and occupation era, to organized protests and boycotts. In some cases, the British met such resistance with military force.[6] It was in this context that the Gambia Company occasionally functioned as a tool of colonial repression, while also affected by greater economic conditions and British policies during the interwar period.

Immediately following its return from East Africa, the Gambia Company suffered personnel problems, similar to what occurred in its early years, as a result of recruiting policies put forth by British officials before the end of the First World War. As noted, the British ramped up recruiting within the Gambia as a means to replace casualties suffered in East Africa and to form an effective reserve force within the colony itself. However, potential plans of WAFF deployment outside of Africa created further demand for recruiting in the Gambia. In June 1918, there were discussions to form a Service Brigade from the WAFF "for eventual service in any theater except against German troops in Europe."[7] British officials noted that there was "no specific date of employment or theater" in mind, but as time progressed, they realized the value the WAFF Service Brigade could provide to the campaign in the Middle East against the Ottoman Empire. The Gambia colonial government, and by extension the Gambia Company, was instructed to form a pioneer company of 250 men, with a reserve of 100-150 men, for attachment to the Service Brigade. The WAFF Service Brigade was planned to consist of one battalion with a Stokes gun battery from the Gold Coast, four battalions of infantry and a battery from Nigeria, and a pioneer company from the Gambia. Interestingly, no WAFF forces were requested from Sierra Leone.[8] Such plans represented a significant departure from British policy concerning African colonial militaries. In the past, African colonial militaries such as the WAFF or the King's African Rifles were only considered for service outside of home territories to the extent that units would help out neighboring colonies in case of emergency, with no possibility of service beyond the African continent. Discussions and plans to send the WAFF to the Middle East showed that British officials were willing to move forward with the creation of an African Imperial Army, and ultimately adopt policies similar to that of the French concerning their *Tirailleurs Senegalais*.[9] The war ended before the WAFF deployed to the Middle East, but plans to do so, on top of the recruiting actions already in place to reinforce the Gambia Company due to its service in East Africa, created a surplus of recruits in the Gambia.

While the Gambia Company was on its return voyage from East Africa, the active reserve force in the Gambia, essentially a second company, was 227 strong with 148 of them training at Cape St. Mary. These figures were on top of the original company and small reserve, minus casualties, returning from East Africa. The normal prewar establishment of the Gambia Company was capped at 128 men.[10] In March 1918, before discussions about the Service Brigade, the War Office instructed the colonial government to stop recruiting in the Gambia.

From the Cameroon campaign until the end of the war, the War Office effectively controlled many aspects of the West African Frontier Force, to include recruiting, which was normally under the authority of the Colonial Office. Governor Edward Cameron, however, argued that such a stoppage would be disastrous to the British military position in the Gambia. First, he did not yet know the state of the returning Gambia Company and its personnel needs; second, the French had recently ramped up conscription within surrounding French Senegal which required increased military presence in the Gambia to stop refugees from entering British territory; third, it would be a convenient time to bring the Gambia Company up to double company organization like every other unit in the WAFF and other British military organizations. Therefore, Governor Cameron kept the inflated numbers of the Gambia Company and continued recruiting until the official end of the war.[11] Although the WAFF was temporarily under the authority of the War Office, the colonial governors were still in control of all locally based military forces within their respective colonies.

With relatively large numbers of recruits already available for the Gambia Company, British officials replaced men who were seen as ineffective or worn out as a result of their service in East Africa and, in some cases, Cameroon. Officials replaced casualties, of which there were a considerable number from East Africa, while a significant number of men were replaced on account of expired terms of service. Through a "weeding process," officials picked through the large numbers of recruits for the best men to serve as replacements in the Gambia Company, while turning away the rest.[12] In effect, officials completely voided the Gambia Company of the military experience it gained during the First World War. By 1921, 70 percent of the Gambia Company had not served during the war.[13] Albeit, it is routine within military organizations that a large proportion of the men are replaced due to various factors after substantial combat operations, but what occurred within the Gambia Company ensured that it was a completely different organization than what it was before and during the war. Not only did it lose the majority of its combat veterans, but the Gambia Company lost its most senior and experienced African NCO,

CSM Ebrima Jalu, who was killed at Nyangao in East Africa, while its seasoned commanding officer, Captain R. Law, left the company in June 1919.[14] Such events created problems for the Gambia Company in the succeeding years.

British officials turning away recruits signaled to the local population that their service was neither wanted nor needed within the Gambia Company. By 1919, recruiting in the Gambia had largely dried up. During the war years, recruiting figures were barely met through cooperation with local chiefs. However now, as was the case before the war, men preferred more lucrative opportunities in the port of Bathurst or agricultural opportunities throughout the protectorate, rather than adhering to the strict military discipline that accompanied service in the Gambia Company. Furthermore, it was perceived that colonial officials did not want their service in the first place.[15] British officials sought to be more selective with the men of the company's reserve force. In 1922, Colonel A. Haywood, now Inspector General of the WAFF, ordered that the Gambia Company be more discriminatory with its reserve force and discharge "any man of over three years of service in the reserve or who is too old."[16] As a result, the Gambia Company's reserve was reduced from 62 to 33 men.[17] Many of the discharged men appeared to be angry and confused by the decision. Governor C.H. Armitage, Governor Cameron's successor, noted:

> *Those so discharged expressed themselves as most dissatisfied and the incident had a bad effect not only on the Reservists themselves but on Recruiting generally, for the discharged Reservists returned to their villages bitterly to complain that they had been dismissed as if they had committed some crime and with no other explanation than that their services were no longer wanted.*[18]

These actions reduced the number of recruits originating from within the Gambia for service with the Gambia Company, just as the company was continuing its transition into an all-Gambian force. As previously discussed, British officials sought greater rates of Gambian military recruiting rather than men from Sierra Leone or surrounding French territory to limit costs, reduce desertions, and ensure a stable reserve force. By 1922, 66 percent of the men within the Company originated from within the Gambia. Although this was a considerable improvement from previous years, the Gambia Company still relied on substantial numbers of recruits originating from outside of the Gambia to fill its ranks. Travelling colonial administrators stepped up their efforts to promote military recruiting throughout the Gambia, especially in the Upper River Province a marginalized region which the British believed housed the most martial men of the Gambia, but only caused a minimal increase in Gambian recruiting.[19]

The substantial loss of experienced men also greatly reduced the military efficiency of the Gambia Company. During annual inspections, the company had considerable difficulties with marksmanship, drill, and tactics while discipline was at an extreme low. In 1919 alone, an astonishing 10 percent of the Gambia Company's strength deserted, presumably to French territory. Colonel Haywood noted that "the company is full of young soldiers and therefore cannot be expected to reach the standard of those units which have a big nucleus of 'veterans.'"[20] Again, as it was in 1902, the blame for the Gambia Company's inefficiency was placed on the African NCOs. From his report in 1922, Haywood argued that "generally the knowledge of drill, powers of observation and instruction shown by native N.C.O's are poor...At present there is scarcely one who is really fit to instruct and lead his section."[21] Like in the Gambia Company's early years, these NCOs had yet to gain the necessary experience and expertise that would make them effective leaders and intermediaries within the company because of their presumably rapid promotion following the war. If any of these NCOs served with the Gambia Company during the war, they most likely did so at the lower ranks and filled empty NCO positions in haste after the company lost the majority of its veterans. The Gambia Company was essentially rebuilt following the war using inexperienced NCOs who needed time to develop their skills. In effect, from the end of the First World War until 1925, the Gambia Company was not considered fit for active service.[22]

Furthermore, British officials effectively blocked the development of a distinct martial identity and culture within the Gambia Company. In 1921, British officers in the Gambia, supported by the governor, petitioned to procure Regimental Colours for the Gambia Company as a means to commemorate the company's exploits during the First World War and raise the *espirit de corps* of its ranks. Although the Gambia Company was an independent unit and therefore had grounds to request its own Colours, the request was denied on the basis that Regimental Colours were given to military organizations of at least battalion size and not individual companies. Colours were seen as central to military culture and identity within the British military system, and signaled independence and distinction from other military units. In fact, other WAFF units were given Colours following the war. By denying the Gambia Company its own Colours, British officials essentially stated that it was not an independent unit with the greater West African Frontier Force, but dependent on other WAFF units, namely the Sierra Leone Battalion, for its military identity, culture, and overall competency. Of course, members of the Gambia Company and the Gambia colonial government viewed matters differently, but the situation showed that the company's actual independence was superficial at best.[23]

As a means to increase the military efficiency of the Gambia Company, British officials discussed the prospects of amalgamation with the Sierra Leone Battalion. In June 1924, officials argued that the amalgamation of the Gambia Company with the SLB would "improve the standard of discipline and increase the military efficiency of the Gambia detachment" in four areas.[24] First, the Gambia Company would train with other SLB companies exposing it to more accurate combat scenarios. Second, the Commanding Officer of the SLB would routinely inspect the Gambia Company and keep watch of its development rather than during just the IG WAFF inspection once a year. Third, officers would cycle between the Gambia Company and other SLB battalion companies and offer fresh perspectives and guidance. Lastly, the SLB would alleviate the Gambia Company's continued recruiting difficulties by providing substantial numbers of Sierra Leonean recruits. In effect, the Gambia Company would be absorbed by the SLB, giving up its own identity and independence, while companies of the SLB would cycle between Bathurst and Freetown to maintain WAFF defense responsibilities in the Gambia.[25]

Although British officials clearly noted that amalgamation would increase the military efficiency of the Gambia Company, there were ulterior motives behind the proposed arrangement. As part of postwar British military reductions in the 1920s, the SLB was reduced to a total of two companies, while the Freetown garrison of the West African Regiment was also downsized and eventually disbanded in 1928. Once the WAR was disbanded, the SLB moved its headquarters and one company to Freetown, while another company remained in the protectorate to maintain internal security there. In effect, these military reductions limited British defensive capabilities at Freetown, especially without the Royal Artillery detachment which also left Freetown in 1928. British officials, particularly in Sierra Leone, hoped that the amalgamation of the Gambia Company with the SLB would give Sierra Leone the much-needed additional military resources to augment its already stretched military forces.[26]

The governor of Sierra Leone welcomed the proposal, assuming that the Gambia colonial government would cover the expenditures required to maintain an SLB company in Bathurst; however, Governor Armitage vehemently opposed the idea. He argued that as Commander-in-Chief of the armed forces in the Gambia he would essentially lose control of his military, while the Commanding Officer of the SLB would never send his most valuable officers and men for service in the Gambia. Additionally, he argued that Sierra Leoneans and Gambians do not mix well socially which would cause contention within the ranks, and the presence of an SLB company in the Gambia, rather than the Gambia Company, might cause friction and anxiety among the local population.

Instead of amalgamation, Governor Armitage proposed that the Gambia Company merge with the Gambia Police to form an armed constabulary to defend the colony. Such a constabulary, he argued, would be effective enough in meeting any internal disturbances with force, while also reducing military expenditure in the Gambia.[27] British officials responded by arguing that the Gambia Company, and all WAFF units, exists for three reasons: for use in the colony in case of internal disturbance, for use in a neighboring colony in case of emergency, and for the protection of the colony in case of external aggression. The formation of a constabulary in the Gambia would void the commitments of the Gambia to a federated military force, the WAFF, while the constabulary would not be of the same military value as the Gambia Company should military force be needed in the Gambia.[28] Governor Armitage's rejection of amalgamation highlights the authority and autonomy that colonial governors held within the military organizational structure of British West Africa. Ultimately, no governor wanted to give up control of his military forces or be dependent on another governor for internal security.

Discussion of amalgamation with the SLB lessened as the Gambia Company increased its military efficiency. By 1925, the company was considered "ready for war" after marked improvement in training and discipline.[29] However, the discussion resumed when the WAR disbandment in 1928 placed further strains on the military situation in Sierra Leone. The following year Governor Armitage, the greatest opponent of amalgamation, was replaced by Governor Edward Denham. British officials then essentially put forth the same arguments they made in 1924 and stiffened their resistance to the idea of a Gambian Constabulary. Colonial administrator J. Hood stated:

> *I have strong views that some troops must be kept in the Gambia as a 'fire extinguisher' for use if there is trouble in the protectorate. Police are not enough in the last resort [sic]. The very sound obligation that a small unit cannot be kept up to date would be met by making it a detailed company of a larger unit.*[30]

These arguments soon lost traction. Both Governor Denham and the Inspector General of the WAFF agreed that the military efficiency of the Gambia Company had improved enough that amalgamation was no longer necessary. They argued "the great improvement in efficiency and recruiting removes the main argument in favour of amalgamation," and there was no need to endure the additional expenses that would come as a result.[31] In effect, Sierra Leone was forced to bear its strained military situation, at least for the time being. Captain J.A. Brawn, OC of the Gambia Company, was given much of the credit for the company's improvement; but credit must also be given to the time needed to foster the military development of the large amount of inexperienced men who constituted the company immediately following the First World War.

The Gambia Company's post war difficulties highlight the personnel problems associated with small, independent military units. Although part of the greater West African Frontier Force, the Gambia Company did not have the luxury of shuffling individuals in and out of its organization to ensure the maintenance of high levels of experience, expertise, and professionalism among the rank-and-file. Where the Sierra Leone Battalion, the Gold Coast Regiment, or the Nigeria Regiment could reassign NCOs and men among its various companies, or battalions in the case of the Gold Coast and Nigeria, and enjoyed a large pool of men to fill empty positions with suitable replacements, the Gambia Company was forced to fill vacancies with fresh recruits with no previous military experience or with men already within the company. In some cases, however, British officers and NCOs were introduced into the Gambia Company after serving with other WAFF units.[32] The Gambia Company's independence ensured that its military efficiency was dependent on maintaining stable numbers of experienced men, which sustained combat operations, casualties, and routine expiration of service periods can disrupt. Ultimately, a few losses within the Gambia Company had a comparably greater impact on military efficiency than it did on larger organizations.

Although by 1925 the military efficiency of the Gambia Company had gradually improved, it still suffered continued recruiting problems that blocked its development into an all-Gambian force. The number of recruits from Sierra Leone was capped at 25 percent of the strength of the company. Throughout the interwar years, the number of Sierra Leoneans serving in the Gambia Company never came close to the prescribed 25 percent, a significant improvement from years past.[33] In fact, it appears that Sierra Leonean recruits were no longer required for service in the Gambia Company after 1935.[34] However, a large proportion of local recruits continued to originate from surrounding French territory. In 1925, 50 percent of the recruits came from French territory, which placed continued limitations on the formation of an effective Gambia Company reserve. The WAFF Ordinance No. 5 of 1924 dictated "every soldier to serve six years with the Colours and three with the Reserve."[35] With continued recruiting of men from French territory, who subsequently returned there upon completion of their service, the Gambia Company Reserve was limited to the soldiers originating from Gambian territory. The reserve did not disappear altogether, but such recruiting practices ensured that the reserve was continually understrength and never met its prescribed establishment of 60 men during the interwar period.[36]

Military recruiting in the Gambia during the 1920s was part of a greater recruiting policy based on imagined martial race stereotypes across the West African Frontier Force. In 1923, Colonel Haywood, Inspector General of the WAFF, released a report on the manpower statistics of martial races throughout British West Africa. In it he argued which ethnicities across the four British West African colonies were the most martial and the number of recruits that could be obtained in peacetime and in the event of WAFF expansion for war. In effect, Colonel Haywood directed that WAFF recruiting should thereafter target specific ethnicities for military service. The report also exposed the high esteem in which British officials held towards the imagined martial races of the Gambia. Of all the West African ethnicities Colonel Haywood discussed, the Jola, Fula, and Serahule were the only ones noted "to make excellent soldiers." Haywood emphasized the connection that Gambian recruits held with the *Tirailleurs Senegalais*, where "these men are much the same type" as the men recruited by the French, showing the fascination British officials held regarding the military efficiency of France's African colonial military.[37]

Furthermore, the diversity of the Gambia Company posed continued problems in the eyes of the British. British officials argued that the lack of military efficiency in the Gambia Company following the First World War was due to the fact that its ranks were made up of sixteen different ethnicities. They believed that such diversity limited effective communication, development, and overall *espirit de corps* in the Gambia Company, and proposed that efforts be made to recruit from only certain "tribes." It is important to note that the term "tribe" expresses racist and colonial connotations within the study of African History, but is maintained in these original quotations to highlight the methods of thought influencing British ideologies of the time. In effect, British officials wished that the Gambia Company resembled other WAFF units "composed of companies [of] which men of the same Tribes can be drafted under Non-Commissioned Officers of their own community." [38] This quote most likely refers to training organizations within the WAFF. At the time, units across the WAFF were becoming increasingly diverse on account of changing recruiting policies and reorganization. Historian David Killingray noted that "During the early years of the WAFF new recruits were placed in 'race companies'...[but] most race companies came to an end in the 1930s and large-scale wartime recruitment led to a great ethnic inter-mixture."[39]

Citing Haywood's previous report, Colonel S.S. Butler, Inspector General of the WAFF, ordered the consolidation of the composition of the Gambia Company in 1926. He directed:

> *I strongly urge that every effort be made to enlist Fulahs and Serahulis [sic] only, with the object in view of having the Company composed entirely of men from these two tribes. I understand that these tribes produce the most satisfactory soldiers and they are already in a majority of the Company.*[40]

Colonel Butler was correct in stating that Fula and Serahule men constituted the majority of the company, but his directive significantly hurt recruiting in the Gambia. Traveling commissioners were instructed to promote military recruiting among Fula and Serahule chiefs only, while the Gambia Company conducted its annual field training in the Upper River Province, a marginalized region of the Gambia, as a means to impress locals and lure them to enlistment.

Significant numbers of recruits among the Fula and Serahule failed to come forward, while other ethnicities were barred from enlistment. As a result, by 1928 the Gambia Company was 20 men understrength, and recruiting was again opened to all local ethnicities with incentives given to chiefs who brought forth recruits to restore the company's strength. Soldiers from the Sierra Leone Battalion were sent to the Gambia in 1928 as a temporary expedient to fix the Gambia Company's manpower deficiency. As a means to improve the military efficiency that British officials believed was lessened from the Gambia Company's "mixed-race composition," officials instead ordered that every man of the company be proficient in English, not just African NCOs. It should be noted that the *lingua franca* of the Gambia Company and the SLB was Pidgin English, while the *lingua franca* of the GCR and NR was Hausa. Such a policy changed with Royal West African Frontier Force expansion just before the Second World War and the adoption of English as the command language across all RWAFF units to ease officer integration within the force. The Gambia Company is unique in that the shift towards English happened much earlier than other WAFF units.[41] In effect, British attempts to target the Fula and Serahule for military recruitment constituted a failed experiment. However, the Gambia was not unique in that the British failed to attract the desired number of recruits from imagined martial races, as outlined by Colonel Haywood, elsewhere in West Africa during the 1920s as well.[42]

British officials also sought greater control over the sexual health of Gambian soldiers during this period. Beginning in 1925, officers were fixated on the presence of sexually transmitted diseases (STD), known at the time as venereal disease (VD), among Gambian soldiers and the effect it had on the military efficiency of the Gambia Company. British officers viewed the presence of VD within military organizations not only as a medical issue, but as a discipline problem. They argued that as a result of poor behavior, soldiers were absent from duty for multiple days while they were being treated for infection at the hospital, which affected training and routine day-to-day operations of the unit.[43] VD had received substantial attention within the British metropolitan Army and dominion forces since the 1860s with the introduction of the Contagious Diseases Acts, which sought to regulate sexual activities and limit the prevalence of VD among soldiers.[44] However, no such initiatives existed within the colonial African forces largely because the British were preoccupied with combating tropical disease, particularly among British personnel. Once the British improved their methods of alleviating tropical disease by the 1920s, their focus shifted to combatting VD among African soldiers.[45]

In an attempt to decrease the prevalence of VD within the Gambia Company, officers conducted surprise "venereal inspections" of every man, sometimes at a rate of once a month.[46] If soldiers were found to be concealing an infection, they were given a "severe punishment" with possible forfeiture of pay, while pay was withheld during a soldier's stay at the hospital.

Furthermore, officers sought to limit soldiers' interaction with "unauthorized women" and pursued improvements in company housing as they argued that "the better accommodation, the better type of woman which the soldier brings into the lines as his wife." VD rates within the Gambia Company ebbed and flowed between the 1920s and 1930s, with the company eventually reaching "deplorably high" figures by 1939.[47] Surprise "venereal inspections" remained a constant occurrence within the Gambia Company during the interwar period.

In the ten years after the First World War, service in the Gambia Company was largely banal, consisting mostly of routine parades and inspections, while the company was under constant criticism from British officials owing to its lack of military efficiency. However, the Gambia Company proved its usefulness to colonial officials, in terms of internal security, during the 1929 Gambian Labor Strike. In 1929, the first Gambian trade union, the Bathurst Trade Union (BTU), formed as a result of severe wage cuts by private sector employers. The BTU, under the leadership of Edward Small, consisted of carpenter, shipwright, and other artisan societies of Bathurst who sought to challenge the widespread wage cuts.

By October 1929, Gambian sailors were on strike protesting the wage cuts; Small called on the BTU to do the same. In the course of three weeks, the BTU achieved significant success. The Gambia Company was first called up to support the civil authorities in the Gambia on 7 November when it took over positions from the Gambia Police, which was required to meet the strikers in force.[49] A heated confrontation between strikers and the Gambia Police began on 14 November, and the police suffered a number of casualties. (it's unclear if the same was true of the strikers).

The colonial authorities were unnerved by the unrest, and so the remainder of Gambia Company was ordered to move by truck from Cape St. Mary to Bathurst to reinforce the police and dissuade any further hostile action by the strikers.[50] The Gambia Company remained in McCarthy Square until the next day, conducting physical training and bayonet drills as a show of force to the local population and strikers, and returned to Cape St. Mary that afternoon. Governor Denham claimed that the Gambia Company's actions "had a great moral effect on the strikers and certainly made the police feel more comfortable."[51] Although brief, this was the first substantial action to counter local protest by the Gambia Company within the Gambia itself in decades.

As a result of the strike, the BTU gained fleeting success. The private sector employers agreed to withdraw the wage cuts, and eventually wages were increased across "all categories of skilled men."[48] The BTU's support grew somewhat, but by 1932 the labor movement in the Gambia quickly became politicized and split into two weaker camps. This division, and the added strain of the global economic depression of the 1930s, limited the success of Gambian labor movements until after the Second World War.[52]

The global economic depression had significant effects on the Gambia Company as well. As a means to save resources, in 1932 the Gambia colonial government ordered that the Gambia Company establishment be reduced by a total of ten people – one British officer, one British NCO, and eight Africans. The reductions in strength lasted until 1937.[53] Additionally, the depression essentially removed any prospects of immediate amalgamation with the SLB. Such an arrangement would require increased costs from transporting soldiers and their families between Sierra Leone and the Gambia and entitlements of extra pay on account of serving outside of home territories.[54] Neither colonial government was willing to endure the additional costs when precious financial resources were needed elsewhere.

Chapter 10
Attachment, Not Amalgamation

THROUGHOUT THE 1930S, THE GAMBIA COMPANY functioned effectively as a military organization and maintained "its well-deserved reputation for smartness, zeal, and efficiency;" a fact that incited great surprise and confusion when in December 1937 the company was informed of its upcoming attachment to the Sierra Leone Battalion. Governor Thomas Southorn informed the company that this would occur by the end of 1938. The company would maintain its own identity and organization; however, it would serve and train in Sierra Leone with other SLB companies, alternating between Bathurst and Freetown every two years.

While the Gambia Company was in Sierra Leone, a SLB company would take up garrison in the Gambia.[55] This announcement caused confusion among the officers and men, because in the past, talks of amalgamation with the SLB were based on the premise that the Gambia Company was an inefficient military organization and amalgamation would cure its deficiencies; but in recent years, this was not the case. For example, the Gambia Company won the 1937 African Cup in marksmanship, signifying the highest standard of weapons training across all British-led African colonial military organizations.[56]

The Gambia Company's attachment to the SLB was part of a greater movement within the British Army to prepare for upcoming war. In 1935, the Italians invaded and conquered Ethiopia. With the intention of stopping further Italian expansion in East Africa, British officials reorganized their colonial forces. In 1928, the West African Frontier Force had received a royal designation and was renamed as the Royal West African Frontier Force (RWAFF).[57] More substantially, RWAFF was also reorganized to aid in the formation of an expeditionary force planned for service in East Africa. Nigeria and the Gold Coast were instructed to form a brigade group for service in East Africa, while RWAFF units from the Gambia and Sierra Leone were to stay in

West Africa for local defense.

Additionally, after the Munich Conference in September 1938, the RWAFF obtained a substantial grant from the British Government for the acquisition of new weapons and equipment. These measures helped facilitate the RWAFF's expansion once the Second World War started.[58] The Gambia Company may have been efficient in recent years as a small independent unit, however the buildup to war exposed its most fundamental problem. As an independent company sized unit, the Gambia Company could never train at the battalion level, limiting the realism of its training and its effective employment in war.

British officials emphasized that these plans called for the attachment of the Gambia Company to the SLB, not an amalgamation of the two. They argued that as a small isolated military organization, the Gambia Company could not conduct training with large numbers of troops and gain an understanding of its place within a battalion during combat operations. Ultimately, the company's time with the SLB was meant to improve its military competency in preparation for upcoming active operations. The plans emphasized that the Gambia Company would maintain a separate identity while with the SLB. Its ranks would continue to be filled by Gambian recruits, not Sierra Leoneans, while the Gambian colonial government would maintain control over finance and administration of the company. However, everything else fell under the authority of the SLB. All military and training matters were directed by the Commanding Officer of the SLB, while the Officer Commanding the Gambia Company was given the same authority as any other company commander within the battalion.[59] In effect, the Gambia Company became just another company of the SLB, albeit with a different name and a chain of administration to a separate colonial government. 'A' Company of the SLB arrived in Bathurst on 7 October 1938 and the Gambia Company left for Freetown three weeks later.[6]

The Gambia Company's first few months in Sierra Leone were full of controversy. Upon arrival in Sierra Leone, Major T.A. Davis, Officer Commanding the Gambia Company, complained that the company's accommodations at Wilberforce in Freetown were poor and clearly neglected by officials. Furthermore, in the weeks following, Major Davis ignored orders requiring the Gambia Company's presence at various SLB formations, inspections, and training sessions. Major Davis was under the impression that the Gambia Company was only sent to Sierra Leone to complete training it could not complete in the Gambia, like large scale maneuvers, while all other matters were still under his control and separate from the SLB.[61]

Major L.H. Bean, Commanding Officer of the SLB, reminded Major Davis that the Gambia Company fell under his authority and served as an active part of the SLB, and was not just attached for training purposes. If it was only there for training purposes, the Gambia Company could just travel to Sierra Leone for a few weeks' worth of training, and subsequently return to the Gambia.[62] Additionally, Major Davis believed that SLB officers were not taking an interest in the wellbeing of the Gambian soldiers. On some occasions, there were heated confrontations between Gambian and Sierra Leonean soldiers, including rock throwing, which confirmed earlier arguments made by British officials in the 1920s about the disdain held between the two groups. Major Davis argued that Major Bean did nothing to correct this behavior and viewed the Gambians as victims of continued discrimination in Sierra Leone. All of this culminated in Major Davis submitting his resignation as the Officer Commanding of the Gambia Company, which was rejected.

Part of this friction could have resulted from the rank and command structures that accompanied the Gambia Company's attachment to the SLB. Although a company commander, Major Davis was given the local field grade rank of major well before travelling to Sierra Leone, while the Commanding Officer of the SLB was also a major, presumably because it was an undersized battalion. This rank structure may have given Major Davis a false sense of security in his attempts to maintain the distinct, independent identity of the Gambia Company while in Sierra Leone, even through outright defiance of orders. Often, field grade ranks given to British officers serving in the RWAFF were considered "local rank," meaning that it was only held while in West Africa and did not translate to their positions within the British units from which they were seconded.[63]

Nonetheless, the response to Major Davis' exploits shows that as a result of attachment to the SLB, the Gambia Company was no longer a completely separate and independent entity within the greater RWAFF. Although British officials actively avoided the terminology, the Gambia Company was essentially amalgamated with the SLB, not simply attached. It was now an active part of the SLB taking part in the defense of Sierra Leone. This is interesting, because under the doctrine of self-sufficiency applied to British colonies, it was assumed that the respective colonial government would control all political, financial, administrative, and military matters within its borders. However, with the Gambia Company's attachment to the SLB, the Gambia colonial government was indirectly financing the defense of Sierra Leone.

The Sierra Leone government was also in turn financing the defense of the Gambia with an SLB company garrisoned at Cape St. Mary; but such a set up raised questions of whether one colonial government contributed more to the scheme than the other, and ultimately, corrupted the doctrine of self-sufficiency.[64] Additionally, this was a unique military situation compared to that in all other British African colonies. As stated in the original WAFF objectives, units would be sent to neighboring colonies in times of emergency, but never to permanently garrison such colonies. This represented a significant change in organization and policy for the WAFF.

The Gambia Company overtly participated in the internal security of Sierra Leone in response to the Sierra Leone Labor Crisis of 1939. Under the guidance of the West African Youth League (WAYL) and I.T.A. Wallace-Johnson, a prominent activist and politician from Sierra Leone, workers protested during the early months of 1939. They were upset with continued low pay scales, poor social policies, and abusive treatment from employers, while colonial administrators failed to negotiate with the various trade unions.[65] From 30 January to 1 March, the Gambia Company and the rest of the SLB were deployed to vital centers throughout Sierra Leone to provide guards, reinforce the police, and restore order as a result of the labor strikes. From 31 January to 20 February, the company guarded the Mabella Coaling Depot, while for the rest of the crisis, it remained on alert to meet disturbances elsewhere.[66] The Gambia Company never found itself in a serious or substantial confrontation with strikers during this period. Although brief, and similar to the 1929 Gambian Labor Strike, the Gambia Company's involvement in the Sierra Leone Labor Crisis highlights the willingness of British officials to use military force in response to labor movements during the interwar period. British officials used both political and military tactics as a means to maintain colonial authority and strict control over African workers. For example, in September 1939 after the crisis, Wallace-Johnson was arrested for "criminal libel" against the war effort and held in prison for the duration of the Second World War so as to not incite further labor unrest.[67]

Additionally, while Sierra Leonean workers conducted their strike, gunners from the Heavy Battery, Royal Artillery positioned in Murray Town simultaneously mutinied on 30 January to improve their conditions of service. The Royal Artillery in Sierra Leone was an imperial unit, separate from the SLB and the RWAFF. In fact, the battery was only recently formed in Sierra Leone in 1937 as part of the revitalization of Sierra Leone defenses and preparation for the Second World War. Since the end of the First World War, the defense structures in the vicinity of Freetown were mostly neglected due to financial cuts. However, in preparation for upcoming conflict, such structures received substantial improvements and new units to man them.

Freetown was considered an important imperial center and port, and thus, received much attention in British preparations for the Second World War. Many of the Royal Artillery personnel were educated Krio who qualified for service in the unit based on their literacy, which was required to train as gunners. However, the black gunners at Murray Town were clearly given worse conditions of service than an all-white artillery unit positioned at Tower Hill. During this period, conditions of service were improved among African soldiers, no matter unit or organization, but there was still a clear disparity between black and white soldiers. Although there is only a vague connection between the mutineers and Wallace-Johnson, it appears that the labor crisis in Sierra Leone was a convenient time for the gunners to openly express their long-standing grievances. The mutiny was brief and largely unsuccessful, while the labor strikes continued for months among various unions with little cooperation.[68]

Although the Gambia Company's attachment to the Sierra Leone Battalion was initially marked by controversy, the 1939 annual Inspector General's report concluded that the move was a clear benefit to both the Gambia Company and the SLB. Major General George Giffard, Inspector General of African Colonial Forces, noted "the military value of both units has materially increased, both from the point of view of internal security and from that of Imperial defense."[69]

It is clear what the Gambia Company gained from the arrangement. Throughout 1939, the company participated in various training maneuvers that it could not accomplish on its own in the Gambia, greatly improving its military competency. Additionally, the Gambia Company acquired new military resources while in Sierra Leone. It was issued new light machine guns as part of the greater rearmament movement—in the past, new armaments took years to find their way to Bathurst—while the Gambia Company enlisted Sierra Leoneans as carriers, who could not otherwise be recruited in the Gambia as the economy offered more lucrative employment opportunities in Bathurst or agricultural jobs throughout the protectorate. In his annual report, General Giffard noted "Carrier enlistment is unpopular. There are no carrier tribes in the Gambia. I recommend the Gambia Company enlists Mendi Carriers while they are in Sierra Leone."[70]

It is less clear what the Sierra Leone Battalion gained from the arrangement. Other than the defense considerations discussed in the next paragraph, the Gambia Company provided no different military capability than 'A' Company of the SLB provided. Rather, British officials argued that the SLB gained better soldiers who, in British minds blurred by martial race ideologies, improved the military efficiency of the SLB. British officials clearly believed that the Gambians held greater martial qualities than the Sierra Leoneans. Giffard argued that a Sierra Leonean soldier does "not come from warrior stock and is excitable and easily led away," while the "physique [of the Gambians] is above the Sierra Leone Battalion and their Native material is good."[71] While the Gambia Company gained tangible military benefits on account of attachment to the SLB, the SLB gained imagined improvement in the quality of its soldiers.

By May 1939, the imminence of war raised questions about defense plans in the Gambia. Under the arrangement dictated by the Gambia Company and SLB reorganization, whatever company garrisoned the Gambia, whether it be the Gambia Company or an SLB company, was to proceed immediately to Sierra Leone to defend Freetown in the event of war. In effect, this arrangement left the Gambia defenseless until reserve forces were called up, trained, and placed in defensive positions. Governor Southorn objected to this arrangement, stating that "The Gambia will have to be sacrificed and left to fend for itself."[72] He argued that when the garrisoned company left for Freetown, no qualified soldiers would be left in the Gambia to train the reserves, while armament for them would be nonexistent.

Furthermore, the Gambia housed a sizable German population on account of a German airliner operating out of Bathurst, which the governor argued, made the town of some import to the Germans. British officials conceded by stating that the company would remain in the Gambia until all Germans were rounded up and confined accordingly, a small number of trained military personnel would remain in the Gambia to train the reserves, and efforts would be made to secure French military support in the event of an attack on Bathurst.[73] In reality, the British did not consider the defense of Bathurst a high priority, or even a priority at all. This arrangement shows that Freetown was of greater imperial importance, but also exposes the true reasons behind the Gambia Company's attachment to the SLB. It may have been to improve the military competency of the Gambia Company on the surface, but the reorganization gave British officials the means to strengthen military positions in West Africa, particularly at Freetown, with the greatest speed in the event of war. Ultimately, bringing the Gambia Company to Freetown in 1938 was a dress rehearsal for possible deployment there during wartime. In the greater British imperial picture, the loss of the Gambia did not matter, while the Gambia Company provided a valuable military resource for the defense of Sierra Leone.[74]

Section Three Conclusion

THE GAMBIA COMPANY EMERGED from the First World War with a positive reputation, but its independence and small size posed serious problems and limited its military efficiency immediately following the war. The state of the company continued to improve, overcoming many of the obstacles that had plagued it since 1902. The Gambia Company no longer enlisted men from Sierra Leone, it maintained a stable, although undermanned, reserve force, and it participated in large scale training maneuvers to gain a better understanding of its place within larger military organizations. Its actual activity during the interwar period, armed responses to labor movements and protests, highlights that the Gambia Company was still a colonial institution tasked to maintain British colonial authority in West Africa. Ultimately, the strategic needs of the British Empire forced the Gambia Company's attachment to the Sierra Leone Battalion and voided its primary responsibility of defending the Gambia in favor of adding much needed military resources to the strategically important imperial center at Freetown.

Regardless of these machinations, with war just over the horizon, the Gambia remained as vulnerable as ever.

Section Four

The Gambia "Company" during the Second World War, 1939-1945

AFRICA WAS THE SCENE of substantial military operations during the Second World War due to its strategic importance as a source of resources and because it lay astride lines of logistics and communication between Europe and Asia. With the fall of France in June 1940, Italy not only sided with Germany, but Italian dictator Benito Mussolini viewed the event as an opportune moment to exploit British vulnerability and expand the Italian Empire in Africa. In the same month, Mussolini launched an ambitious offensive into British East Africa (today's Kenya), British Somaliland (today's Republic of Somaliland), and Anglo-Egyptian controlled Sudan. The East Africa campaign required the service of Indian, South African, East African, and West African soldiers to protect British strategic interests, particularly the Suez Canal and the Red Sea, ultimately initiating Africa's extensive involvement in the Second World War.[1]

Historian Ashley Jackson argues that "the war greatly enhanced Africa's value in the eyes of its colonial rulers."[2] Africa not only contributed massive amounts of resources that fueled war production, subsequently furthering economic exploitation of the continent, but provided the various imperial powers with vast numbers of men to fight in distant campaigns. As in the First World War, African soldiers were sent throughout Africa, to Europe, and other corners of the world to support the imperial defense of their colonial rulers. However, this time it was on a much grander scale.[3]

The Royal West African Frontier Force rapidly expanded in the Gambia and greater British West Africa during the Second World War. However, the Gambia was placed in a peculiar position and was highly vulnerable on account of being completely surrounded by Vichy controlled French West Africa. Furthermore, through military expansion, the Gambia maintained disproportionate obligations for imperial defense compared to the rest of British West Africa. Nonetheless, Gambian soldiers were sent to Southeast Asia in support of British strategic interests. While in Burma (today's Myanmar), the 1st Battalion of the newly formed Gambia Regiment effectively supported Allied operations to push the Japanese out of the British territory, relieve the territorial threat to India, and reopen the Burma Road to supply China.

Analyzing the Gambian experience during the Second World War not only exposes the lowest levels dynamics of the conflict, but shows the importance to the overall war effort of the lesser known theaters of the war.

Chapter 11
The Vichy Threat

THE FALL OF FRANCE TO THE GERMANS had major implications for the political, and eventually military, environment in Africa. The French Republican government was toppled and replaced by the collaborationist regime headed by Henri Phillippe Petain at Vichy. At the time, France held three substantial territorial federations in Africa – French North Africa (FNA), French West Africa (FWA), and French Equatorial Africa (FEA). North Africa and FWA quickly fell under the Vichy sphere, while French colonial administrators in FEA, minus Gabon, rallied for the Free France cause of Charles de Gaulle. Additionally, French mandated Cameroon sided with Free France while Madagascar remained Vichy. FEA's move towards the Free France camp was extremely important because it gave de Gaulle legitimacy and a territorial base from which to continue his resistance against the Vichy Government and German occupation of France.

Ultimately, French Equatorial Africa had little choice but to side with Free France. De Gaulle and his Free French Forces took shelter in London and maintained the political and military support of the British Government. FEA was essentially surrounded by British or Allied controlled territories, which meant economic isolation if it did not cooperate with the Allies. Felix Eboue, the black governor of Chad, was instrumental in securing Free French control of FEA. Although the economic incentive was important, Eboue rallied to the Free France cause to combat the "discriminatory nature" of the Vichy government. Chad was the first to announce its split from Vichy control, with the majority of FEA following suit. North Africa and French West Africa, on the other hand, had greater freedom of movement due to port facilities and their closer proximity to Europe that they fell under the protective umbrella of Vichy and, by extension, the Germans.[4]

As stipulated in its armistice with Germany, Vichy France was allowed to keep French colonies in Africa "so long as they remained neutral and the armies stationed in them were reduced in size."[5] Pierre Boisson, former Governor-General of French Equatorial Africa, quickly travelled to Dakar and imposed Vichy rule over all of French West Africa. As outlined in the conditions of the armistice, Boisson declared that he would resist German interference in FWA, but also protect FWA against any military intervention in the region, whether it be from the British, Gaullists, Italians, or Germans. In effect, Boisson declared Vichy FWA as a neutral territory. However, even with this declaration, the British remained uneasy about German influence over the Vichy Government and Germany's desire to reestablish itself as an imperial power in Africa.[6] In fact, Vichy colonial administrators enacted policies to substantially increase the labor force in FWA in order to provide resources for the Axis war effort. However, through blockades and cooperation with neutral African territories, the Allies were able to limit African resources from falling into Axis hands while the Allies themselves continued to exploit African labor and resources to achieve the greatest level of production yet seen in colonial Africa.[7]

Anglo-Vichy relations were initially strained by Vichy's collaboration with the Germans, but subsequent events added further controversy. In early July 1940, the British sank the French fleet at Mers el-Kebir off the coast of French Algiers to prevent the ships from falling into German hands. The attack destroyed almost all of Vichy's naval resources while killing close to 1,300 French sailors. Furthermore, the British and Free French Forces launched the failed amphibious invasion of Dakar, Operation Menace, on 23 September. Although de Gaulle maintained the support of French Equatorial Africa, he wanted to increase his resources and support by capturing French West Africa for Free France. The British, on the other hand, viewed Vichy control of FWA, particularly the port of Dakar, as a great threat to their African territories. If under German control, Dakar could be used as a base of naval operations against British sea routes to Freetown and the Cape.

The British hoped that a pre-emptive strike on Dakar would ensure that West Africa did not become a major theater of the war. Free French Forces and the British acted on faulty intelligence and inflated estimates of anti-Vichy sentiment to execute a bombardment and subsequent amphibious invasion of Dakar. The affair became a "debacle" with unexpected Vichy warships arriving on scene, a dense fog severely limiting bombing accuracy, and the fact that the anticipated uprising against Vichy rule never materialized.[8] After the defeat, de Gaulle traveled to Brazzaville in French Equatorial Africa to continue the Free France movement. By November, Free French forces captured Gabon with the help of the Royal Navy, and finally secured control over the entirety of FEA. Additionally, in May 1942 the Allies launched an amphibious invasion of Madagascar to ensure that the island did not transfer from Vichy to Japanese control and threaten the rest of the Indian Ocean. In July 1943, Free France also secured French West Africa following the Allied invasion of North Africa, Operation Torch.[9]

All of these incidents only strengthened the British fear of Vichy military reprisal and German control over Vichy affairs. British West Africa, the Gambia in particular, was a convenient place where the Vichy regime could seek revenge. The Gambia, a small sliver of land completely surrounded by French West Africa, was an easy target for a Vichy military response, while the other British West African territories also shared borders with FWA. In fact, after the failed attack on Dakar, the Germans allowed Vichy to expand the forces in FWA that had been reduced following the armistice. With these expanded forces, Vichy FWA developed plans to invade the Gambia on 28 October, 1940 that never materialized.[10]

In order to defend their West African territory, the British sought to strengthen and expand their military footing in the region. In June 1940, Lieutenant General George Giffard, previously the Inspector General of the African colonial forces, was named as General Officer Commanding (GOC) West Africa under direct orders from the War Office. All military forces in British West Africa, including the Royal West African Frontier Force, now fell under the operational control of the War Office, which created West Africa Command (WAC), headquartered in Accra in the Gold Coast. Much like during the First World War, the governors essentially lost control of their colonial military forces, retaining it only for purposes of internal security. After his appointment to command WAC, Giffard continued the actions he took as Inspector General of African colonial forces just before the war to better prepare the RWAFF for active operations.[11] Between 1940 and 1941, the RWAFF expanded to unprecedented levels and entirely new support units were formed.

Chapter 12
Expansion

THE VICHY THREAT ULTIMATELY CHANGED British strategic imperatives in West Africa and forced an unprecedented expansion of the Royal West African Frontier Force. The Nigeria and Gold Coast Brigades were deployed in June 1940 for active service against the Italians in the East Africa campaign. This left the Sierra Leone Battalion, the Gambia Company, and relatively small detachments of Gold Coast and Nigerian units to defend British colonial holdings and the strategically important port at Freetown. Eventually, the deployed brigades returned to West Africa in late 1941, but in the meantime, British officials set out to expand and reorganize the RWAFF in order to deter the previously unforeseen Vichy threat.[12] The Gambia Company, garrisoned in Freetown, returned to Bathurst in early August 1940 by a Polish ship, the *S.S. Cieszyn*.[13] This was a significant change to British military defense plans for West Africa, as Gambian resources were intended to immediately contribute to the defense of Freetown in the event of war. However, this plan was based on the premise that France would be an ally in such a war and that French West Africa posed no territorial threat to the Gambia. The defense of Freetown was still of priority to the British, but now the Gambia received greater consideration than it was previously given.[14] Additionally, other military forces arrived in Freetown, which allowed the Gambia Company to resume defensive responsibilities in the Gambia.[15]

Before the Gambia Company returned to Bathurst, British officials took steps to increase the establishment of the military forces in the Gambia to a battalion level. Reserves were called up and officials set out on a substantial recruiting drive throughout the entirety of the protectorate. In the South Bank Province alone, 225 men enlisted for military service in August 1940. In total, over 1,000 Gambians enlisted to serve as soldiers, auxiliary personnel, and small numbers of carriers in 1940, though not all were accepted for service due to physical restrictions. Recruiting during this initial drive was relatively easy. Men were eager to enlist and chiefs were willing to meet quotas given to them by British officials; however, when recruiting was ramped up again in 1941, enthusiasm had waned.[16]

The original Gambia Company, the reserves, and a large number of new recruits now constituted the Gambia Battalion. Many members of the Gambia Company were promoted to more senior ranks and dispersed across the four companies of the Gambia Battalion to provide experience and expertise for the newly formed sub-units.[17] However, with such a large proportion of fresh recruits, the Gambia Battalion needed time to develop its military competency. As a result, 4th Battalion of the Gold Coast Regiment (4 GCR), which did not see service in East Africa, arrived in the Gambia to augment the Gambia Battalion in October 1940. While the Gambia Battalion trained intensively at Cape St. Mary, 4 GCR garrisoned a newly constructed camp in the village of Brikama.[18] The presence of two infantry battalions in the Gambia posed a new and substantial deterrent to the Vichy territorial threat.

In 1941, before talks of RWAFF deployment to Southeast Asia, British officials sought to further expand the military forces in the Gambia and establish a stable influx of recruits to replace any casualties to be suffered in combat operations. British officials called for the immediate recruitment of over 800 soldiers, auxiliaries, and carriers, essentially forming a second Gambia Battalion, and eventual recruitment of an additional 500 men for units not yet authorized. The 1st and 2nd Gambia Battalions now constituted the Gambia Regiment. In addition, officials noted that the Gambia would need to enlist almost 50 recruits per month for replacements. Officials in the Gambia argued that such figures could not be reached without some form of conscription or, in the least, changes to established recruiting practices.[19]

In previous years, British officials targeted certain ethnicities for military recruiting based on martial race ideologies, but failed in creating a homogenous organization of a few select "martial races" within the Gambia Company. The British maintained preferences, which is why the Fula and Serahule constituted large numbers of the Gambia Company rank-and-file, though authorities still recruited from numerous other ethnicities within the Senegambia region.

Spurred by the increased demand for recruits, such preferences were abandoned in the Gambia, and the rest of British colonial Africa, during this new period of military expansion. The British Empire needed as many men as possible to support imperial defense within Africa and elsewhere. For instance, West Africa Command required more soldiers to serve as infantrymen, but also educated personnel to serve in medical, artillery, pioneer, signals, and other specialized roles. Previous military recruiting based on martial race preferences targeted marginalized peoples with low education levels, but this practice was no longer sustainable. Furthermore, such racially based policies were becoming increasingly unfashionable and hypocritical in the face of Nazism. Thus, military recruiting during RWAFF expansion looked significantly different than it did in the past.[20]

Through the quota requirements given to local chiefs, the Mandingo (Mandinka) now constituted the greatest number of military recruits, ahead of the Fula and Serahule, on account of being the largest ethnic group in the Gambia.[21] Additionally, physical restrictions like height requirements were dropped to increase the number of available men in the Gambia. Even these changes were not sufficient to generate the expected number of recruits, and so conscription remained on the table.[22]

In this second wave of recruiting, some Gambians were hesitant to enlist because of the potential for them to be tasked as carriers, who were paid less than soldiers with worse conditions of service. Gambians were extremely averse to serving as carriers, mainly because they had better paying labor opportunities available to them in the Gambia that did not require them to be subjected to military discipline. There were persistent rumors that if they did enlist, they would be forced to serve as carriers, rather than soldiers.

The presence of 4 GCR added further hesitation among Gambians. While at Brikama, 4 GCR needed laborers and carriers, which were to be supplied by the local population. One British official noted, "Service as carriers for a non-Gambian Battalion is probably the most unpopular of all forms of military service among the Gambians."[23] Relative to the requirements for infantry personnel, the number of carriers needed from the Gambia was extremely small. Before resorting to conscription, which had recently been instituted in the Gold Coast, British officials instead hoped to find success through new recruiting tactics.[24] These included the promotion of competition among local chiefs, giving soldiers local leave to promote military service among their contemporaries, and embellishing military service through films and posters.[25] In fact, much of the wartime propaganda used within British West Africa was a replication of what was used in Europe and drew on discourses of freedom and "Imperial idealism." Some historians argue that although this propaganda strengthened Africans' sense of belonging within the greater British Empire and fostered wartime support, it had a "paradoxical effect" on the politics of decolonization following the war.[26]

There was great aversion to conscription in the Gambia among British officials mainly because of the desire to draw an ideological difference with

Vichy West Africa. British officials wanted to maintain the image among West Africans that British colonial rule in the Gambia was a force for good, and was better and more humane than French colonialism. Of course, such a claim by British officials was one sided and declared from a position of power, but the British did have a clear advantage over the French in that they had never before resorted to military conscription in West Africa. Since 1912, the French established universal conscription throughout their West African territories to maintain a large colonial African army for overseas campaigns, including within Europe.[27] With an essentially opposite policy concerning African colonial militaries, the British had not pursued such large-scale military recruitment which necessitated conscription in West Africa. British officials argued that Senegambians preferred British rule over French rule on account of conscription. One British official noted:

> *It is strongly felt that [conscription] would place a severe strain on the loyalty of the Gambians, it would rob them of their most highly prized advantages over their French-African neighbours and it would provide Vichy with the finest propaganda it could desire.*[28]

The British feared that conscription would corrupt the "loyalty" of the Gambians and provide Vichy France the means to improve its own image in West Africa. However, there was also a labor argument against the implementation of military conscription in the Gambia. By 1941, the value of Gambian laborers was of increasing importance due to wartime conditions. The Gambia's imports were severely limited, which necessitated increased food production throughout the protectorate. Furthermore, the "strange farmers" from French territory, who normally formed a substantial part of the seasonal agricultural labor force, could no longer cross into the Gambia to work. Military conscription, British officials argued, would greatly reduce the Gambia's productive capacity when Gambian workers were needed the most.[29]

British officials in the Gambia ultimately detested raising the military establishment in the colony after the initial recruiting drive in 1940, whether through conscription or voluntary means, because of the unfair commitments the Gambia was asked to fulfill compared to the rest of British West Africa. At the time, the Gambia's population was around 200,000 people, by far the smallest of any colony in all of British West Africa. The recruiting drive of 1941 called for the enlistment of 1:125 of the Gambia's population into military service. By comparison, military recruiting in 1941 in Nigeria called for 1:1050 of its population, with the Gold Coast and Sierra Leone at 1:350 and 1:300

respectively. One British official noted that, based on population, the raising of two battalions in the Gambia was the equivalent of raising 200 battalions in Nigeria.[30]

Despite the misgivings of officials, the Gambia contributed a disproportionate amount to Royal West African Frontier Force expansion between 1940 and 1941. Military conscription, officials argued, would not only corrupt Gambian "loyalty," improve the Vichy image, and significantly affect Gambian labor output, but it would further the Gambia's already unfair obligations to the British West African military establishment. Eventually, in 1942, a system of partial conscription was introduced in the Gambia to procure enough laborers to work at the docks and in pioneer units; while military recruitment was still executed through a quota system in cooperation with local chiefs.[31] However, British officials did conduct "round-ups" of all unemployed males in Bathurst to enlist them into military service. In one instance in early 1945, about 400 individuals were brought in during a nighttime "round-up." Of these men, 250 were found to be fit to serve, 150 of whom subsequently deserted months later.[32]

Full military conscription was never established in the Gambia partly because British officials filled the Gambia's manpower requirements with recruits from French territory, a continuing practice of past military recruitment in the Gambia. British officials made greater attempts to entice French subjects to cross into Gambian territory and join the RWAFF. The exact number of recruits from French territory is unknown, but it was noted that 2nd Battalion Gambia Regiment (2 GR), which remained in the Gambia for the duration of the war, maintained a large number of French subjects in its ranks.[33] In fact, this posed a significant problem once control of French West Africa transitioned to Free France. French officials requested that French subjects leave their British units and return to French territory to serve as soldiers in the French Army. Of course, the British were hesitant to give up whatever soldiers were in their ranks, so by June 1944 British officials declared they would no longer enlist men from French territory, but not necessarily repatriate large numbers of French subjects serving in British uniforms. At times this situation turned contentious, with reported incidents of British subjects from the Gambia being forcibly impressed into French military service while visiting French territory.[34]

The expansion of the Royal West African Frontier Force also impacted the composition of its leadership. Beginning in 1941, a large number of Polish and white Rhodesian officers were introduced into the officer corps of the RWAFF. One of the biggest problems associated with RWAFF expansion, and discussed extensively before the war, was the ability to obtain enough British officers and

NCOs to serve in command and training positions. Before the war, British officials made substantial efforts to establish European reserves throughout colonial enclaves in British West Africa to serve as officers and NCOs in the event of RWAFF expansion, but even that was not enough to alleviate the inevitable European manpower deficiency. With the fall of Poland in October 1939, hundreds of Polish officers were sent to Scotland and sat idle waiting for attachment to British Army units. General Giffard petitioned the War Office to allow the Poles to serve as officers in the RWAFF, which would solve his manpower deficiencies and ensure the continuation of racial hierarchies within the force rather than resorting to giving commissions to Africans. Only a small number of Africans were given commissions during the Second World War, with Lieutenant Seth Anthony of the Gold Coast being the first in 1942. As noted, Africans were previously barred entirely from receiving commissions in British-led colonial militaries. Lt. Anthony's commission represented a significant policy change regarding African officers, which continued after the war through the process of Africanizing the colonial militaries in preparation for Independence.[35] In total, over 250 Polish officers served with the RWAFF, however, only a very small number of Poles accompanied the West Africans to Burma. In the Gambia alone, twenty-four Polish officers served with the two Gambia battalions, five of whom accompanied 1 GR for active operations in Burma. The majority of the Poles, like the majority of African soldiers, did not know English and resorted to Pidgin English, which had a long history of use as a trade language in West Africa.[36]

Additionally, white Rhodesian officers were invited to serve in the RWAFF.[37] During the First World War, the all-white infantry battalion of the Rhodesia Regiment suffered disastrous losses during the East Africa campaign. With the Second World War, there was a tendency not to form military units solely from small communities to avoid repeating disasters similar to what befell the Newfoundlanders at Beaumont Hamel during the Battle of the Somme.[38] As such, men from the small population of white Southern Rhodesians were dispersed throughout various British military organizations, with the RWAFF being just one destination for white Rhodesian officers. Additionally, there was the myth among British military circles that white Rhodesians possessed experience and skill in leading black soldiers. To the contrary, the Rhodesians were infamous for often expressing their racist beliefs while serving with the West Africans. Unlike in Southern Africa, West Africa did not have the type of settler colonialism that produced extremely blatant expressions of racism by European colonizers. While serving with the RWAFF, the Rhodesians continued their habits of outright racism and discrimination towards African soldiers. These new officers did create some tension within the RWAFF, but the tension ultimately did not detract from the Poles' and Rhodesian's purpose—to aid in the training of a rapidly expanded force and maintain the racial hierarchies within its command structures.[39]

The massive expansion of military forces in the Gambia also caused numerous internal disturbances. The sheer size of the new RWAFF military establishment in the Gambia, two Gambian battalions and one Gold Coast battalion, was unprecedented and led to feelings of insecurity among the local population and heated confrontations with soldiers. In November 1941, the most significant disturbance occurred in Brikama, where 4 GCR was garrisoned. One Gold Coast soldier was killed as a result of an argument in the central market, which in turn caused a large group of soldiers to revert to "mob rule" to track down anyone they believed was involved in the killing, creating chaos throughout the whole village. The event not only exposed Gambian insecurity, but also the discontent felt by the Gold Coast soldiers due to being permanently garrisoned in a foreign land.[40]

There were also confrontations between Gambian soldiers and the local population. On several occasions between 1941 and 1944, Gambian soldiers were charged with inciting unrest, assault, and arson, among numerous other charges related to their interactions with villages in close proximity to their posts.[41] In addition to this tension with the local population, there was considerable friction between Gambian soldiers and the Gambia Police. The two organizations often quarreled over the boundaries of military authority in the Gambia, while soldiers were upset when the police did little to investigate grievances brought to them. In one case, "police lines were looted and burned by a crowd of soldiers" after the police refused to investigate thefts suffered by the soldiers.[42] Such instances highlight the social problems associated with maintaining a large, idle military force in a relatively small populated area.

The Gambia Regiment maintained a unique religious composition among its soldiers when compared to other Royal West African Frontier Force units units during the Second World War era. The Gambia Regiment was an outlier in terms of religion in that it was largely Muslim, due to the sustained predominance of Islam in the Gambia. In the past, other RWAFF units maintained a majority of Muslims within the rank-and-file, which gradually transitioned into a mix of Muslims and traditionalists. However, with new religious trends in West Africa before the war and the onset of wartime military expansion, RWAFF soldiers became increasingly Christian. Despite these changes within the greater RWAFF, the Gambia Regiment maintained a majority of Muslims in its ranks following expansion. Within the Gambian military establishment,

Christians and traditionalists were no longer represented in significant numbers when recruits stopped arriving from Sierra Leone in 1935.[43] Furthermore, spiritual beliefs and religion were a key component in the martial culture of the Gambians. Gambian soldiers often carried with them or wore elaborate ju-jus for protection while in combat, a common practice throughout West Africa and often used during warfare. Soldiers carried ju-jus to protect themselves from injury or death, while also to help cure their comrades who became casualties in battle. As Muslims, Gambian soldiers practiced the Islamic adaption to the West African tradition by placing folded up prayers from the Quran wrapped in cloth in their ju-jus.[44]

By late 1942, the Vichy threat to British West Africa had largely subsided with the success of the Allied landings in North Africa, which freed up the RWAFF for active service elsewhere. In December, General Giffard recommended to the War Office that the RWAFF could be used for active operations in Burma against the Japanese.[45] Based on racial stereotypes, British officials argued that African soldiers were highly qualified for service in Burma because of the belief that they were more adaptable and better prepared for bush fighting than other Allied soldiers. In fact, such beliefs were very far from the truth. One British officer who served with the Gambians in Burma noted, "Africans, in the Gambia at least, did not go into the thick bush...The jungle in Burma was as unfamiliar to them as it was to Europeans."[46] Nonetheless, the discussions and eventual authorization to send West Africans for active service outside of Africa signaled a significant departure from previously discussed British policies concerning African colonial militaries.[47] By January 1943, the War Office ordered the formation of two infantry divisions from RWAFF units—the 81st and 82nd (West African) Divisions—for service in Burma. In March, the 81st (WA) Division stood up, composed of three brigades—the 3rd, 5th, and 6th (WA) Brigades. The 4th Battalion Nigeria Regiment (4 NR), the 1st Battalion Sierra Leone Regiment (1 SLR), and the 1st Battalion Gambia Regiment (1 GR) constituted the 6th (WA) Brigade. By July, the 81st (WA) Division was en route to Burma.[48]

With 1 GR slated for active operations in Burma, 2 GR remained in the Gambia for defense duties. After the recruiting drive of 1941, 2 GR formed and was garrisoned in the vicinity of Denton Bridge. Eventually, 2 GR took over the military camp at Brikama and 4 GCR returned to the Gold Coast for coastal defense there in 1943.[49] Some British officers commented that the officers of 2 GR were "rejects" and "mediocre," which translated to poor training regimens for their soldiers.[50] However, 2 GR was given a different task than 1 GR after 1942. Its mission was to defend the Gambia against an unlikely

Vichy attack, which became increasingly unlikely after 1942.[51] Additionally, 2 GR was tasked to provide and train replacements for 1 GR in Burma. In fact, 1 GR's deployment to Burma added further demands for military recruitment in the Gambia to replace expected casualties. In March 1943, the monthly requirement of recruits increased from 48 to 75 men through an increase in the quotas given to local chiefs. Such figures were reluctantly met until July 1944 when British officials initiated a reduction of the RWAFF units performing defense duties in West Africa, and so military recruiting in the Gambia could be significantly reduced.[52]

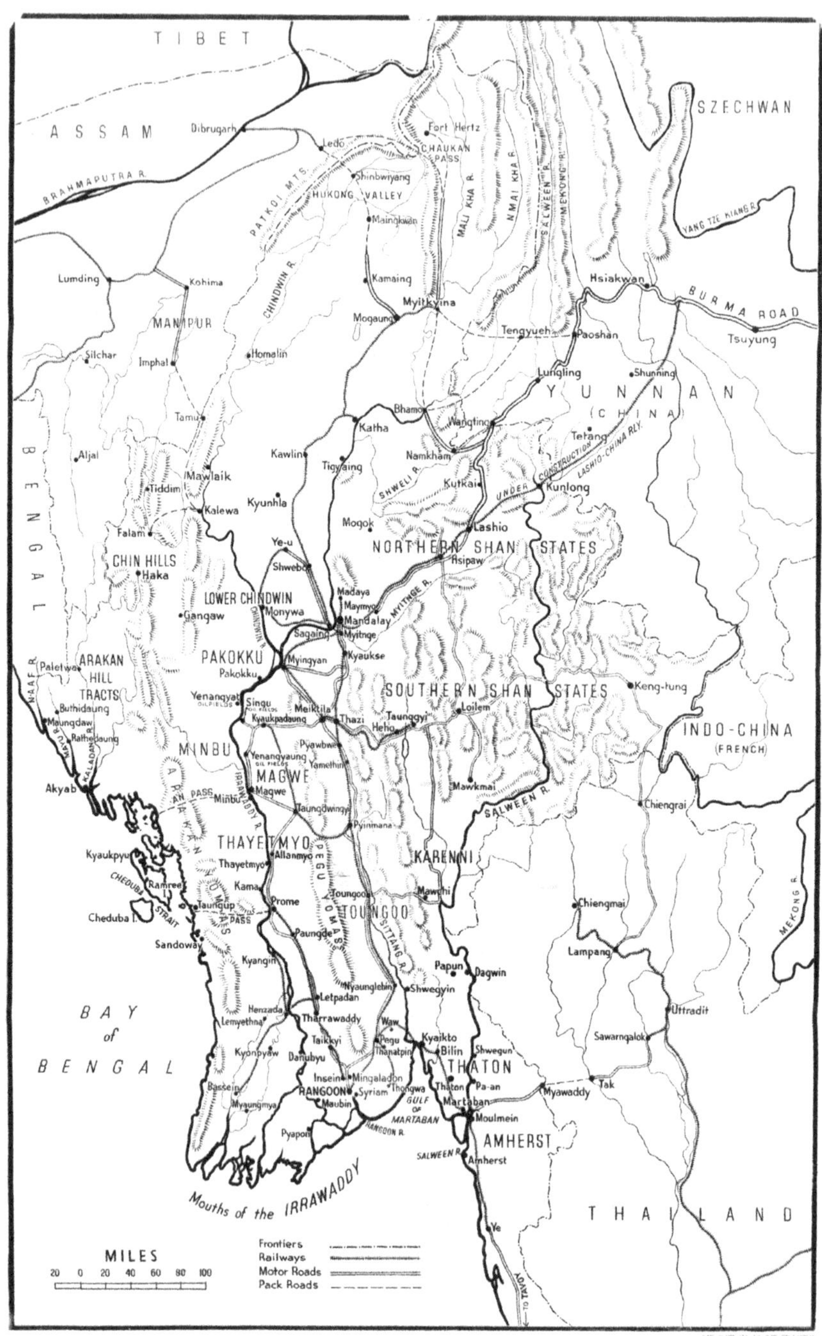

TIBET
ASSAM
SZECHWAN
Dibrugarh
Ledo
Fort Hertz
CHAUKAN PASS
BRAHMAPUTRA R.
PATKOI MTS.
Shinbwiyang
HUKONG VALLEY
Maingkwan
MALI KHA R.
NMAI KHA R.
SALWEEN R.
MEKONG R.
YANG TZE KIANG R.
Lumding
Kohima
CHINDWIN R.
Kamaing
Myitkyina
Hsiakwan
BURMA ROAD
Mogaung
MANIPUR
Tengyueh
Paoshan
Tsuyung
Silchar
Imphal
Homalin
Lungling
Shunning
YUNNAN
(CHINA)
Tamu
Bhamo
Wanting
Katha
Tetang
Namkham
LASHIO-CHINA RLY.
UNDER CONSTRUCTION
BENGAL
Aljal
Kawlin
Tigyaing
SHWELI R.
Kutkai
Kunlong
Mawlaik
Tiddim
Kalewa
Kyunhla
Mogok
Lashio
Falam
Ye-u
NORTHERN SHAN STATES
Hsipaw
CHIN HILLS
Haka
Shwebo
LOWER CHINDWIN
Madaya
Maymyo
MYITNGE R.
Monywa
Mandalay
Gangaw
Sagaing
Myitnge
ARAKAN HILL TRACTS
Paletwa
NAAF R.
PAKOKKU
Pakokku
Myingyan
Kyaukse
Yenangyat
OILFIELDS
Singu
Meiktila
SOUTHERN SHAN STATES
Keng-tung
Buthidaung
Maungdaw
MAYU R.
Rathedaung
KALADAN R.
Kyaukpadaung
Thazi
Heho
Taunggyi
Loilem
INDO-CHINA
(FRENCH)
MINBU
Pyawbwe
Yenangyaung
OIL FIELDS
Yamethin
MAGWE
Akyab
AN PASS
Minbu
Magwe
IRRAWADDY R.
ARAKAN
Taungdwingyi
Mawkmai
SALWEEN R.
Chiengrai
Pyinmana
THAYETMYO
Allanmyo
KARENNI
Kyaukpyu
Thayetmyo
PEGU YOMAS
CHEDUBA STRAIT
Ramree I.
Kama
Toungoo
Mawchi
Taungup
PASS
Prome
TOUNGOO
Chiengmai
MEKONG R.
Cheduba I.
Sandoway
Paungde
SITTANG R.
Lampang
Kyangin
Papun
Dagwin
Nyaunglebin
Shwegyin
Letpadan
BAY
of
BENGAL
Henzada
Lemyethna
Tharrawaddy
Waw
Uttradit
Taikkyi
Pegu
Kyaikto
Sawarngalok
Kyonpyaw
Danubyu
Thanatpin
Bilin
Shwegun
THATON
Insein
Mingaladon
Thongwa
Tak
Bassein
RANGOON
Syriam
Thaton
Pa-an
Myawaddy
Myaungmya
Maubin
GULF OF MARTABAN
Martaban
Moulmein
Pyapon
RANGOON R.
AMHERST
SALWEEN R.
Amherst
Mouths of the IRRAWADDY
THAILAND
Ye
TO TAVOY
MILES
20 0 20 40 60 80 100
Frontiers
Railways
Motor Roads
Pack Roads

Chapter 13
Operations in Burma

THE JAPANESE INVASION OF BURMA ultimately precipitated out of an obsession with China. Burma, a British colony administratively separate from India since 1937, shared its northeastern border with China. Japan invaded eastern China in 1937, and since then had been focused on eliminating the Western supported government of Chiang Kai-shek, who had been pushed to Western China, near Burma. Chiang and his Chinese nationalists forced the Sino-Japanese conflict to a stalemate largely through American and British logistical support by means of the Burma Road. Through Burma, the Allies supplied Chiang to further overstretch and distract Japanese Imperial Forces to the point that Burma, an otherwise insignificant target for Japanese objectives, except possibly for natural resources, became a strategic imperative to defeat China. Japan invaded Burma in early 1942, initially capturing Rangoon (Yangon), and established control over the entire region by the end of 1943. The Japanese invasion was a great disaster for the British, who retreated towards the Indian frontier.[53]

To retake Burma and diminish the Japanese threat to India, the Allies launched an ambitious offensive in late 1942. British and Indian forces attempted to advance into the Arakan, the western region of Burma, and capture the strategically vital town of Akyab. Simultaneously, the Chindits, special operations units of the British and Indian Armies trained for long range jungle penetration led by Major General Orde Wingate, sought to advance south on a separate front after crossing the Chindwin River. Both operations failed and sent the Allies searching for new plans to alleviate the increasingly perilous state of affairs in Burma and India.[54]

By mid-1943, the 81 (WA) Division had massed in Lagos, Nigeria and begun training for the bush warfare operations expected in Burma. Major General Christopher Woolner, commander of the 81 (WA) Division, noted that the "training of units had been uneven in their different Colonies and in many cases unsuitable for jungle operations." In fact, there was no established doctrine of jungle warfare for the Royal West African Frontier Force. Before embarking for India, Woolner directed that the 81 (WA) Division, especially its British officers and NCOs, undergo jungle warfare training in the Nigerian bush; however, "time was lacking" and the men who did receive training were often rushed through it. Instead, Woolner hoped that such jungle training could be completed while the division was in India.[59]

The Gambians and the rest of 81 (WA) Division's 6 Brigade left Nigeria on 10 July by ship and arrived in Bombay on 14 August after passing through Cape Town. The entire 81 (WA) Division camped in the vicinity of Bombay for almost two months waiting for its move across India and eventually towards Burma. Having arrived first in India, 6 Brigade had the benefit of receiving more jungle training than the rest of the 81 (WA) Division. Suitable jungle and mountainous terrain was found about 80 kilometers from Bombay where the division completed company and battalion training.[60] It should be noted that the all-Nigerian 3 Brigade trained in West Africa as an "all-weather and all-terrain Mobile Infantry Brigade...earmarked for Special Operations in Burma." As a result, upon arriving in India, 3 Brigade was sent to join Wingate's Chindits for operations near the Irrawaddy River in central Burma.[61] For the entirety of its time in Burma, the 81 (WA) Division was without the service of 3 Brigade, functioning only with two brigades.

The Allies decided on an invasion of Burma beginning in late 1943 along three general fronts. The Chinese invaded from the north through Kamaing, Britain's IV Corps on the central front near the Chindwin River, and Britain's XV Corps through the Arakan area. Both the IV and XV Corps formed the Fourteenth Army under South East Asia Command (SEAC). The 81 (WA) Division, with small detachments from the Indian Army and the King's African Rifles, was destined for the Arakan as part of XV Corps. Against the 81 (WA) Division were the Japanese 55th Infantry Division and elements of the 54th Division as support. Differences in military organization between the Japanese and the British made the size of the 55th Infantry Division larger than that of the 81 (WA) Division.[55]

The Arakan region was crucial because its provincial capital, Akyab, housed a valuable airfield from which the Japanese could launch air attacks against India; but conversely, if in Allied possession, could be used for air raids against Japanese held Rangoon to the south. Furthermore, the Arakan offered a convenient overland route for a possible Japanese invasion of India, as it is the western most province of Burma with access to port facilities and efficient resupply by way of the Bay of Bengal. India became increasingly vulnerable with growing nationalist movements and resistance among Indians against British authority, which consequently required military responses by British soldiers who might be used for defending the Indian Frontier or operations in Burma. Interestingly, the Arakan is the present-day Rakhine State of Myanmar, home to Myanmar's Muslim minority, the Rohingya, and site of ongoing sectarian violence. In fact, Muslims of the Arakan were predominately pro-British compared to their Buddhist counterparts, as they sought colonial protection from the religious violence that affected the region just before the war.[56]

General William Slim, commander of the Fourteenth Army, ordered that the 81 (WA) Division form the right flank guard of XV Corps' advance down the Arakan. Slim instructed that the 81 (WA) Division advance down the extremely isolated Kaladan Valley to distract the Japanese, easing the resistance facing the main XV Corps front, while also threatening the east-west communication lines of the Japanese.[57] Specifically, they were to "advance down the [Kaladan] valley to capture Kyautaw with the ultimate objective of cutting the Htizwe-Kanzauk road – the enemy's main communication between the Kalapanzin and Kaladan Valleys."[58] The nature of these orders, and the environment in which the West Africans were tasked to fight, ensured they were almost entirely isolated from other Allied units in Burma, arguably more isolated than the famed Chindits under General Wingate. By a combination of rail and sea, the division travelled to Calcutta and eventually to Chiringa (in present-day Bangladesh), the divisional staging point, before advancing towards the Kaladan Valley in early December.[62]

In order to get into the valley, the 81 (WA) Division first needed to construct a 120-kilometer jeep track over steep hills and vicious terrain, called the "West African Way." Largely without any roadmaking machinery, the division built the track in two months and was funneling into the Kaladan Valley by mid-January 1944. However, the "West African Way" was by no means a sustainable overland supply route for the 81 (WA) Division. It crossed four ranges of steep hills and was susceptible to washouts by monsoons that plagued the region for months on end.[63]

The Arakan's geography created a logistical nightmare for a modern army. Its terrain includes dense jungle overgrowth, a multitude of hills and valleys, and knife edge ridges two to three thousand feet high – such terrain features allowed for easy concealment of Japanese machine gun and artillery positions, especially at ambush points. Roads connecting population centers were nonexistent; rather, a maze of game trails offered the most efficient means of travel through the dense jungle. Major rivers, such as the Kaladan, and smaller streams were not bridged and subject to massive flooding during Burma's six-month monsoon season—which offered little transportation value to the West Africans and posed considerable difficulties when crossings were required.[67] Furthermore, diseases such as malaria and typhoid ran rampant in the jungle. Similar to their experience in East Africa during the First World War, the West Africans appear to have been more resistant to the tropical diseases of the Arakan compared to other Allied forces fighting in Burma. In fact, the British developed a comprehensive medical system to combat malaria in Burma, with the introduction of anti-malarial drugs, to better protect Allied forces.[68]

The way in which 81 (WA) Division solved the problems posed by the dense jungle was unique—it became the first military unit in history to be supplied entirely by air. Sustained aerial supply, of course, was only possible due to Allied air supremacy over Burma; yet, air operations were still constrained by weather and terrain conditions. Supplies were dropped by parachute, but hastily constructed airfields were required for larger supply loads and the evacuation of casualties. As a result, the 81 (WA) Division's operations in the Arakan were often constrained by the need to find suitable terrain for airfield construction and efficient collection of dropped supplies.[64]

Although there were some constraints, sustained aerial supply gave the West Africans a high degree of mobility and flexibility in operations against the Japanese. They could move in the jungle, often on a "one-man frontage" through extremely complex and narrow game trails, without the worry of having a long supply train in tow. The Auxiliary Groups of the 81 (WA) Division added even greater mobility. Similar to conflicts in the past, the RWAFF relied on a large number of carriers while in Burma. In fact, the application of carriers in military operations was a staple of West African warfare that British officials viewed as a great benefit for operations in the dense Arakan jungle. Carriers collected air-dropped supplies, cleared airfields, and distributed supplies throughout the 81 (WA) Division with impressive speed.

Initially, carriers were unarmed, but most were given small arms, and, in some cases, reassigned as infantrymen as the campaign progressed. Carriers not only gave the division a high degree of mobility and a logistical advantage over the Japanese, but also created a deeper infantry reserve while the division was isolated in the Burmese jungle. Historian F.A.S. Clarke describes the RWAFF's logistical advantage as such; "The use of carriers by West African formations in the hill jungles of Burma made them far more mobile than those relying on mules or other transport and, when supplied by air, remarkably flexible."[65] The benefit of such a logistical setup ensured that the West Africans would not be bogged down when they were required to pursue the enemy, or retreat into the jungle. Since air supply operations were routine, soldiers travelled light, only with essential equipment and minimal rations to last until the next expected drop—usually every three days. Additionally, the evacuation of causalities from small airstrips allowed for even greater freedom of movement in such an isolated setting. Much of the 81 (WA) Division's success against the Japanese in Burma was due to its impressive mobility.[66]

The geography, carrier use, and aerial supply all ensured that the 81 (WA) Division operated in the Arakan largely without artillery support. While the West Africans had the advantage in mobility over the Japanese, they were at a disadvantage in firepower. The 81 (WA) Division fought without medium machine guns and 2-inch mortars (which were preferred over 3" mortars), while the divisional artillery detachment was limited to twelve 3.7" mountain guns with a slow rate of fire and no penetrating power. On some occasions the division could call in airstrikes, both bombing and strafing missions, but such strikes were often inaccurate and unreliable. One platoon commander of 1 GR noted that the first and second Kaladan Campaigns were "almost entirely an infantryman's war, with rare and usually ineffective interventions by artillery of small calibre and aircraft."[69] On the other side, the Japanese held highly concealed and effective artillery and machine gun positions that posed considerable problems for the West Africans. Ultimately, the nature of the geography in the Arakan ensured that the tactical advantage was on the side of the defense, who could rely on carefully constructed positions. However, once these positions were discovered and taken out, the nature of combat transitioned to one of close-quarter bush warfare, with ranges sometimes as close as ten meters, where the West Africans held the advantage.[70]

1 GR arrived in the Kaladan Valley on 18 January 1944 and started its advance southwards on the west bank of the river, initiating the First Kaladan Campaign. By 22 January, 1 GR took the village of Paletwa, which was previously held by the Japanese. The battalion experienced little opposition, except a small ambush which cost three Gambian casualties the day before, as the Japanese made no real attempt to hold Paletwa and fled. In fact, neither the West Africans nor the Japanese placed defensive positions or camped in the immediate vicinity of small Burmese villages, compared to larger administrative centers in the Arakan, largely because they offered so little protection. Rather, the Japanese, and to some extent the West Africans, set up concealed defensive positions surrounding various villages. For about a week, 1 GR cleared Japanese patrols out the area immediately surrounding and south of Paletwa. Soon the division received reports that a substantial Japanese force was positioned near Kaladan village and 6 Brigade, including the Gambians, advanced south along

both banks of the Kaladan on 1 February.[71]

The Gambians remained on the west bank of the Kaladan, while 1 SLR advanced on the east bank to find suitable terrain for an airstrip, and were ordered that "if they could not destroy the enemy in Kaladan village they were to 'invest the enemy in area Kaladan-Grankhazi.'" Beginning on 7 February, 1 GR attacked Japanese positions surrounding Kaladan village, particularly to the southwest of the village. However, the attack essentially turned into a siege of the village with the Japanese staunchly holding on to their positions and the Gambians making little progress. On the first day, D Company eventually occupied the village after a short mortar bombardment on Japanese positions, but withdrew on account of the other Gambian companies failing to secure their right flank. Over the next two days, the Gambians failed to make any further advances on the village against effective concealed Japanese positions and constant harassment from a Japanese medium machine gun nicknamed "Kaladan Sam."

By 10 February, the first airstrike given to the 81 (WA) Division sought to loosen up Japanese positions around Kaladan village, with three Hawker Hurricanes delivering two bombs apiece, but the strike did not hit any Japanese bunkers. The division's three Light Batteries of mortars arrived the next day to support the Gambians, which did soften up Japanese positions and effectively helped the Gambians gain control of the village. By 12 February, the Gambians were "investing" in their positions in the vicinity of the Kaladan and Grankhazi villages, but such positions did not cover the south and southwestern flanks of the two villages. For the time being it did not matter, because the Japanese retreated during the night. The siege of Kaladan village cost the Gambians nine killed and thirty wounded. The majority of the casualties originated from D Company, whose attack had temporarily been so successful.[72]

After being momentarily held up in taking Kaladan village, 1 GR and the rest of 6 Brigade advanced southward along the Kaladan River towards the 81 (WA) Division's first objective, Kyauktaw. Like Paletwa, Kyauktaw was an important administrative center that offered valuable infrastructure for river crossings. 1 GR set off from Kaladan village and reached the junction of the Pi Chaung, a smaller river, and the Kaladan River on 19 February. At the junction, 1 GR came under fire from a small Japanese position in the vicinity of Petu. 1 GR's 3" mortars bombarded the Japanese position, which gave the Gambians enough cover to cross the 200-meter span of the Pi Chaung in *khistis* (wooden canoes) and collapsible assault boats. Once 1 GR crossed the river, they found the area vacated by the Japanese and on 24 February they entered Kyauktaw unopposed. The Japanese had withdrawn because on 19 February, 4 NR had captured Pagoda Hill, a long feature that gave dominating views of Kyauktaw from the opposite side of the Kaladan River. In effect, "anyone who held this hill could make Kyauktaw untenable." While 1 GR occupied Kyauktaw and 4 NR strengthened its positions on and around Pagoda Hill, 1 SLR and the East African Scouts, who recently joined the 81 (WA) Division, constructed an airstrip for C-47 Dakota transport aircraft at Medaung, on the east bank of the Kaladan.[73]

The situation around Kyauktaw remained steady for about a week until on 26 February General Woolner received new orders. He was directed to move 5 and 6 Brigades southwest towards the Mayu River to block any Japanese lines of communication between Akyab and Buthidaung, while also keeping the Japanese guessing as to the 81 (WA) Division's main objective in the Arakan. However, Woolner was also instructed that the Japanese "MUST NOT [*sic*] be allowed to est[ablish] himself at KYAUKTAW under any circumstances."[74] As 6 Brigade discovered in taking Kyauktaw, in order to hold the village, Pagoda Hill must be secured, "which could scarcely be done by less than a brigade" in the event of a Japanese offensive. By the 28th, all of 6 Brigade crossed the Kaladan and were positioned on the west bank of the river, which left the East African Scouts at Thayettabin, about 6 kilometers west of Pagoda Hill, as the only unit defending the hill.[75]

On 1 March, while 5 Brigade was in the south near Apaukwa, two Japanese battalions of the 55th Division counterattacked to retake Pagoda Hill with the intention of capturing Kyauktaw. The Japanese shelled the East African positions at Thayettabin, which pushed the East Africans back to defensive positions on Pagoda Hill. At the time, 1 GR, positioned at Ponnaywa, constituted the reserve of the entire 81 (WA) Division which was stretched thinly from north of Kyauktaw to Apaukwa. B Company, 1 GR crossed the Kaladan early on the 2nd to reinforce the East Africans and were followed later in the day by the rest of the battalion. By dusk, the Gambians reached the East Africans and were given the order "to hold Pagoda Hill at all costs."[76]

1 GR arrived at Pagoda Hill to find only a "skeleton" East African unit which was "inexperienced and having suffered many casualties in their withdrawal against the advancing Japanese."[77] Lieutenant Colonel George Laing, commander of 1 GR, dispersed the four Gambian companies in defensive positions on and around the hill; one company placed on top of the hill, one placed in reserve at the foot of the hill adjacent to the Kaladan River, and two companies placed in forward positions left and right of Pagoda Hill. Throughout the night, the Gambians endured intermittent bombardment from Japanese artillery. Soon Laing received reports that the Japanese were "streaming past"

the left forward position in large numbers, having surprised the now overrun and out of contact D Company.[78] The Japanese quickly overwhelmed the rest of 1 GR positions, having found their way in between and behind Gambian lines. Defeated, Laing issued orders for a general retreat and to re-cross the Kaladan River to safety. After their capture of Pagoda Hill, the Japanese were hesitant to continue their offensive. Lieutenant John Hamilton, a platoon commander and signals officer of 1 GR, noted:

> *Just before we pulled back after the rest of the battalion, I saw Japanese on the top of Pagoda Hill. I did not fire at them, as they showed no sign of firing down at us, and it seemed senseless to tempt them; strangely, they did not fire a shot all the time that three companies and HQ were getting out to the south.*[79]

Hamilton ultimately argues that although the battle of Pagoda Hill was a clear defeat for the Gambians, the affair brought minimal gain for the Japanese. They could have easily caused greater damage to the retreating 1 GR, but because of a "lack of orders or initiative," or possibly weakened by casualties suffered from Gambian defenses, the Japanese were content with securing control of the strategically important Pagoda Hill without continuing with further attacks.[80]

The retreating elements of 1 GR withdrew to the south and west towards the Kaladan River while General Woolner considered plans for a counterattack to retake the hill. 1 SLR was sent over the river as reinforcements, but found itself stranded on a sandy flood plain not outlined on British maps, which delayed their crossing. Eventually, all of 6 Brigade was ordered back to the west bank of the Kaladan after moving north to secure a safer crossing. As a result of the hurried and disorganized retreat, a large contingent of D Company 1 GR was left behind Japanese lines on Pagoda Hill, finding their way back to the battalion some three weeks later.[81]

Although 1 GR was considered "temporarily out of action," which influenced General Woolner's decision not to launch a counterattack, the battalion surprisingly suffered relatively few casualties from the action on Pagoda Hill. Its defensive positions were so spread out that the Japanese easily filtered into the gaps and overran the hill rather than engage a head on assault against the Gambians. 1 GR suffered eight killed and thirty wounded, which was substantially lower than casualty figures for the East Africans, who received the brunt of the Japanese attacks of 1-3 March and lost about one quarter of their total strength.

Ultimately, the loss of Pagoda Hill was seen as a strategic "disaster" for the

81 (WA) Division. The attack on the hill by two Japanese battalions was part of a greater Japanese counterattack of five and a half battalions against the West Africans to retake Kyauktaw. The West Africans' overall strategy in the Kaladan Valley was simply to "remain a force in being" to distract the Japanese forces in the Arakan. The loss of Pagoda Hill, and the subsequent loss of Kyauktaw made that strategy extremely difficult since Kyauktaw was an important administrative center and valuable location in the valley. General Woolner decided to withdraw the 81 (WA) Division north along the west bank of the Kaladan to give the West Africans the opportunity to rest and regroup for an eventual counterattack on Kyauktaw.[82]

The Japanese pursued the 81 (WA) Division's retreat north. By 12 March, the 81 (WA) Division made its way to Kyingri where the Pi Chaung forms a convenient "loop" perfect for defensive positions. In the Kyingri Loop, the West Africans constructed a Dakota airstrip to evacuate casualties suffered since the loss of Pagoda Hill and receive much needed supplies and reinforcements. On 18 March, the whole of 5 Brigade was in the loop, with 6 Brigade scattered in defensive positions and 1 GR north of the loop at Wanbanhla. During this time, various patrols were sent throughout the surrounding area to get in touch with the Japanese, but it appeared there was no immediate intention by them to make an advance on the Kyingri Loop. Instead, the Japanese intermittently shelled West African positions with a 75 mm. gun, causing no casualties. On 25 March, General Woolner received orders to leave the Kyingri Loop and advance to the Kalapanzin Valley, effectively abandoning the Kaladan Valley. With the 81 (WA) Division in the Kalapanzin Valley, it could form a substantial threat to the left flank of any Japanese advance north from Taung. Additionally, the move to a less hostile Kalapanzin Valley would give the West Africans much needed rest after almost ten weeks of constant combat operations. However, General Woolner was instructed to leave one battalion in the Kaladan Valley to deceive the Japanese into thinking that an advance down the Kaladan was still a possibility. That battalion was 1 GR.[83]

By this time there was a slight reorganization within the regiment. The lost elements of D Company had finally returned to the battalion by 27 March, but now the whole company was convinced that they were cursed. The chaos following Pagoda Hill was just the latest in a longline of bad fortunes that had plagued them. The company's quartermaster sergeant accidentally killed himself when he dropped his Sten gun during an inspection in September 1943, the company was victim to a nasty cholera outbreak, and they had suffered a disproportionate number of casualties during the action in Kaladan village. 1 GR officers decided to exchange all of the soldiers of the company with other soldiers of the battalion and rename it "X Company" with platoons numbered 18 to 20. The reorganization eased Gambian concerns.[84]

As the 81 (WA) Division advanced west towards the Kalapanzin Valley, 1 GR remained in the Kaladan Valley with the Indian units of the 7th Battalion of the 16th Punjab Regiment and 1Tripura Rifles under Lieutenant Colonel John Hubert, forming "Hubforce." Hubforce was given three tasks:

> *First, to protect the three columns which were evacuating the MT [motor transport], the guns, the non-urgent sick and the unwanted personnel; second, to try to persuade the enemy that the whole division was still in the Kaladan and preparing to move forward again to threaten Myohaung; third, to prevent the enemy from infiltrating northwards.*[85]

The Gambians joined Hubforce on 9 April and took up positions near Kaladan village. The Japanese were soon pressuring Hubforce's flanks around the village, which initiated a general retreat northward by the Gambians and Indians. 1 GR passed through Paletwa and took up a defensive position in the vicinity of Labawa on 1 May. By 10 May, the Japanese launched substantial attacks against the Gambians at Labawa with fresh reinforcements. Again, Hubforce retreated north to defensive positions on Frontier Hill in the vicinity of Mowdok. Against further attacks, the Indians withdrew north of Mowdok on 14 May, leaving the Gambians on Frontier Hill defending Mowdok from the south.[86]

In many respects, Mowdok was considered a "gateway to India" for its access to mountain passes and the Mowdok-Baungprei track leading there, and Hubforce sought to hold it for as long as possible. From 14 to 20 May, 1 GR remained on Frontier Hill resisting constant attacks from Japanese patrols. The company in the forward position of the hill, under the command of Captain David Cookson, beat off "three major and six minor Japanese attacks" alone during the strenuous week.[87]

The story of one Gambian soldier within the company sheds light on the demanding nature of operations in the vicinity of Frontier Hill. Positioned in the forward sector of the hill, Private Musa N'Jie was wounded by a mortar fragment during a Japanese attack. Although wounded, Private N'Jie continued to man his light machine gun until his company had defeated the attack. At the aid shelter, Private N'Jie was informed that he would be evacuated because of his wounds, but protested and returned to his platoon "saying he had a gun to look after." He returned to the same position on the same machine gun where he was just recently wounded, and "continued to fire with accuracy and determination during several further attacks."[88] Private N'Jie's actions not only show the tense situation facing the Gambians at Frontier Hill, but it also shows the strength of Gambian resolve in the face of a determined enemy.

On the 20th, Indian units took over Frontier Hill and the Gambians withdrew to positions just north of Mowdok. With the Indians facing increasing Japanese pressure and giving up some ground, the Gambians were called up on the 24th to launch a counterattack against newly established defensive Japanese positions. Compared to the action that the Gambians previously experienced in the Kaladan Valley, their counterattack on Frontier Hill brought them within meters of Japanese positions. For instance:

> *Private Bokari Bojan was leading a scout of the leading section [of the attack when] he got within 10 yds. of an enemy bunker position without being seen and then engaged the enemy with grenades. When the remainder of the platoon were held up by enemy fire and grenades, Pte. Bojan went back to his platoon and collected a small party of men. With these men, he again climbed the hill under heavy fire and hurled grenades into the enemy bunker.*[89]

The Gambians did not gain much ground against the larger and concealed Japanese forces, and by the 27th the Japanese controlled all of Frontier Hill. As a result, Hubforce practically garrisoned Mowdok against potential Japanese attack in order to maintain control of the valuable village. Lieutenant N.D. Poulsen of 1 GR explained that at Mowdok the Gambians were as isolated as they ever were in the Kaladan Valley. He noted that "Apart from Wingate's first Chindit expedition, I believe that we must have been further from medical attention beyond the competence of a regimental MO [medical officer], than any other troops in the British forces."[90] The area around Frontier Hill and Mowdok offered no suitable location for the construction of an airfield, nor did Hubforce have time to construct such an airfield as they were under constant Japanese attack. Casualties were inefficiently sent down river towards Thanchi on *khistis*, while supplies were airdropped when possible. Similar to Pagoda Hill, Mowdok and Frontier Hill were scenes of substantial 1 GR operations where the Gambians were forced to retreat against aggressive Japanese attacks.[91]

By this time, both sides were concentrating their forces in "monsoon positions" for the coming rains which effectively limited substantial offensive action. After 1 SLR arrived in Mowdok on 5 June to relieve Hubforce, both 1 SLR and 1 GR moved towards Thanchi on the Sangu River, while the Indians moved towards Tranchi, as there was apparently no further Japanese threat to Mowdok. However, on 11 June, the Japanese captured Mowdok from 1 Tripura

Rifles who were left to defend the village. 1 GR and 1 SLR made minor advances back towards Mowdok with the intention of a counterattack, but ultimately settled in their respective monsoon positions once the rains started on 15 June. The Gambians were positioned at Bandarban, the closest location to Japanese positions in the Kaladan Valley, by 17 July. This marked the end to the First Kaladan Campaign.[92]

Although Hubforce, including the Gambians, ultimately lost Mowdok, it was successful in its objective of deceiving the Japanese about Allied intentions in the Kaladan. After 11 April, the Japanese essentially lost contact with the greater 81 (WA) Division and followed the trail left by Hubforce, thinking that it "was the tail of the Division." After their capture of Pagoda Hill, the Japanese could not gather a large attacking force, even of battalion strength, against the 81 (WA) Division or Hubforce. The Japanese pursuit consisted of small, widely spread-out parties which, in effect, offered little resistance to the West African retreat to the Kalapanzin Valley and north in the Kaladan Valley. Additionally, although the 81 (WA) Division essentially abandoned the Kaladan Valley, it was somewhat successful in its mission. Its rapid advance down the Kaladan, with 5 Brigade reaching as far south as Apaukwa, concerned the Japanese and drew substantial reinforcements from the 55th and 54th Divisions. This eased the situation facing the XV Corps on the main front in the Arakan.[93]

During the monsoon months, the West Africans largely rested, but also conducted small patrols to check Japanese movements. Neither side was willing to launch a large-scale offensive while the rains made the land impassable and supply extremely difficult. On 18 August 1944, the 81 (WA) Division, now under the command of Major General F.J. Loftus Tottenham, received orders to return to the Kaladan Valley when the rains ended and advance south with the intention of distracting, and hopefully destroying, Japanese forces in the Arakan to ease the central front of the Fourteenth Army and facilitate an amphibious landing at Akyab. After substantial supply preparations during September, the West Africans began moving into the Kaladan in early October to start the Second Kaladan Campaign.[94]

6 Brigade, including the Gambians, was given the task to capture the first objective in the division's push into the Kaladan Valley to take Mowdok and Frontier Hill. 1 GR formed the spearhead of the Brigade's advance to take over the Singpa area from 5 Brigade, which was ordered south of Mowdok towards Topui. With 1 GR at Singpa, 1 SLR and 4 NR advanced on Mowdok, taking the village with little opposition by 9 October. However, Frontier Hill proved to be more difficult for the Nigerians and Sierra Leoneans. 1 GR moved to Mowdok, while 1 SLR and 4 NR advanced on the hill. After numerous airstrikes

on Japanese positions and constant patrols by the West Africans, the hill was taken by the 17th. With 6 Brigade firmly established in the Mowdok area, and 5 Brigade successful in its operations to the south, the 81 (WA) Division was given its next objective to advance south and take Paletwa.[95]

The advance towards Paletwa commenced on 1 November. The Gambians led 6 Brigade's advance south. They relieved 5 GCR of 5 Brigade at Sepeo, then continued south along the Pi Chaung towards Satwei, where they encountered minor resistance. As the advance guard, the Gambians were tasked with uncovering Japanese defensive and artillery positions that might attack the West Africans from the rear. The Gambians were quite successful in this task, with the exploits of Lance Corporal Samba Jallow as a case in point. On 15 November, Lance Corporal Jallow "wormed his way" forward almost 300 meters, to within 20 meters of a Japanese mortar position, armed only with a grenade, to report on the location. Two more times during the day, Lance Corporal Jallow discovered Japanese positions alone in a similar manner to accurately direct Gambian mortar fire on the Japanese, which brought considerable loss to the Japanese and no losses to the Gambians. Lance Corporal Jallow epitomizes how advances in the Kaladan Valley truly did occur on a one-man front.[96]

1 GR remained at Satwei until 16 November, when it joined the general concentration at Auklo for an eventual attack on Paletwa. 5 Brigade advanced on Paletwa, and 6 Brigade were ordered to take Kaladan village. 6 Brigade, including the Gambians, advanced south without substantial opposition. It took Kaladan village on the 28th and continued to Orama by 4 December. After taking Orama, 6 Brigade was ordered across the Kaladan River near Tinma. This crossing of the Kaladan River, like many others, was highly dangerous for the Gambians. There was no reconnaissance of Japanese positions on the opposite bank, so Captain Jan Zieleznik, a Polish officer, and Lance Corporal Yaryah Jallow first crossed the river in a *khisti* to report on the Japanese and establish a safe bridgehead for the crossing. In the middle of the night, the two men crossed the 500-meter expanse of the river to find no Japanese defensive positions. Soon, a Japanese patrol opened fire on the men, and Lance Corporal Jallow returned fire with his Bren gun, defeating the attack and ultimately securing a safe crossing for the rest of 6 Brigade. Similar events occurred throughout the entirety of the Kaladan Campaigns, which show the vulnerable nature of river crossings that the Gambians needed to complete in order to continue their advances.[97]

While the rest of 6 Brigade maintained the bridgehead in the vicinity of Tinma, 1 GR was sent to a defensive position near Sanon, almost 5 kilometers southeast of Tinma. On the 15th, the Japanese launched a substantial battalion strength counterattack to push back the West Africans. 5 Brigade largely bore the brunt of the unsuccessful attack, but the Gambians were involved. The Gambians suffered shelling and defeated the initial dusk attack of the Japanese, who subsequently shifted their attack against 5 Brigade positions.[98]

After shoring up its positions around Tinma, the 81 (WA) Division moved east to link up with the Yan Chaung, the river it would follow to continue the advance south. On 17 December,1 GR formed the vanguard for the division's advance to the Yan Chaung. It went well, Lieutenant John Hamilton saying that, "the advance of 1 GR down the Yan Chaung was, by the standards of jungle war, quick and easy."[99] The battalion advanced against small Japanese patrols and dugouts, often taking the Japanese by surprise. In one instance on the 19th, near the village of Kaingyi, Private Kinti Kamara single handedly overwhelmed a Japanese dugout and was awarded the Military Medal. His award citation reads:

> *While crossing open farmland south of the village, Pte Kamara's section came under heavy fire from an enemy dug-in position. Without hesitation, firing his Bren Gun from the hip, Pte Kamara charged the enemy position across 200 yards of open paddy. The enemy concentrated LMG, rifle, and grenade discharger fire on him, but totally disregarding personal safety, he continued his charge. In face of this deadly persistence the enemy abandoned his positions and fled in confusion.*[100]

With meager opposition put up by the Japanese and impressive feats like that of Private Kamara, the Gambians suffered very few casualties in their advance down the Yan Chaung. By 21 December, 1 GR reached Thandada and remained there until the 30th. While at Thandada, 1 GR dispatched continuous patrols to secure the area. One patrol reached Pagoda Hill, where the battalion had retreated in the face of a staunch Japanese counteroffensive only months prior in March, to find the area completely clear of the Japanese.[101]

The 81 (WA) Division's rapid advance south in the Kaladan Valley and the 82 (WA) Division's advance along the Mayu River facilitated the unopposed amphibious invasion of Akyab by the 25th (Indian) Division. The West Africans advanced in such force, that the Japanese viewed them as the greatest threat to their positions in the Arakan and withdrew three battalions protecting Akyab to stop the West Africans. On 3 January 1945, Akyab was captured by the 25th (Indian) Division, whose commander commented that "the battle for Akyab had been won in the Kaladan valley." With Akyab taken, the Allies decided to advance on Myohaung, the last major Japanese stronghold in the area, with the intention of forcing the Japanese to order a general retreat from the Arakan. The 81 (WA) Division initiated its advance on Myohaung fromthe north in early

January, while the 82 (WA) Division advanced on the town from the west.[102]

From Thandada, 1 GR advanced south to a position in the vicinity of Ma Kyaze just north of another river, the Ngashwe myaung. At this position, the Gambians received constant shelling as they waited to cross the river and suffered some casualties. Private Dudu N'Dowe was instrumental in facilitating this dangerous river crossing by swimming after loose assault boats and untangling the guide ropes stretched across the river, all under heavy Japanese fire.[103] By 10 January, the Gambians were across the Ngashwe myaung as 1 SLR overran Japanese positions just south in an area called "Starfish." After 5 Brigade made substantial progress against Japanese positions in the vicinity of Kwazon, they initiated a general withdrawal towards Myohaung. The Gambians proceeded down the Ngashwe myaung and reached Myaukswe on the 21st unopposed. The Gambians continued south and joined the rest of 6 Brigade in an area west of Myohaung on the 26th as reserves for the final assault on Myohaung. However, 6 Brigade and the Gambians played no immediate part in the Battle of Myohaung. 5 Brigade and elements of the 82 (WA) Division overwhelmed the Japanese and captured the town on 24 January, pushing the Japanese south with the 82 (WA) Division in pursuit.[104]

By this time, the tide was beginning to turn against the Japanese within Burma and elsewhere. The Americans were making advances in the Pacific, while American bombers began strategic bombing operations over Japanese cities and industrial targets in the summer of 1944.[105] In Burma specifically, the Fourteenth Army made substantial advances on the Central Front, crossing the Irrawaddy River near Mandalay. Such events surely softened up the Japanese defense of Myohaung and facilitated an easier capture of the town.[106]

The Battle of Myohaung is said to be "the greatest concentration of force ever achieved by the RWAFF."[107] The battle consisted of two infantry divisions with soldiers representing all four British West African colonies. Myohaung marked the end of the Second Kaladan Campaign and was the 81 (WA) Division's last action in Burma, and ultimately, for the duration of the war. The 82 (WA) Division relieved the 81 (WA) Division and continued operations against the Japanese in the Arakan. After being relieved, the 81 (WA) Division marched out of the Kaladan Valley for the last time and eventually were moved to Chiringa for much needed rest.[108]

From the West Africans' perspective, the Second Kaladan Campaign was by far a great improvement from the first. The morale of the West Africans was much higher, the complex logistics of sustained aerial supply were improved, and the West Africans had a better understanding of the ground on which they were tasked to fight. In the end, the 81 (WA) Division suffered only a third as many casualties as they sustained in the First Kaladan Campaign and achieved greater successes. Although the 81 (WA) Division did not participate in its capture, Akyab was of extreme value for the Allies. It offered a valuable airfield and an important staging area for upcoming operations further south in the Arakan and greater Burma. The 81 (WA) Division's advance in the Kaladan facilitated the capture of Akyab and eased the situation facing the central front in the Arakan. The Burma Campaign ultimately continued until just before the end of the war when the Japanese retreated to Malaya after losing Rangoon in May 1945.[109]

Much credit for the 81 (WA) Division's success in the Kaladan Valley should be given to 1 GR. The Gambians routinely found themselves as the vanguard to divisional or 6 Brigade advances, while also being called on to relieve units in distress. They faced a substantial Japanese counterattack at Pagoda Hill, the largest of the First Kaladan Campaign, and served as a valuable part in the highly vulnerable and risky operations of Hubforce. Even during the "interval" of the two Kaladan campaigns in the monsoon months, the Gambians conducted constant patrols from Bandarban as the closest unit to the Japanese, while the rest of the 81 (WA) Division safely recovered at Chiringa.[110] Again, as they did from operations in Cameroon and East Africa during the First World War, the Gambians built a favorable reputation as a result of their exploits in the Burma Campaign.

Chapter 14
Demobilization

THE GAMBIANS ONLY REMAINED AT CHIRINGA for a short time. In mid-March 1945, the 81 (WA) Division moved to the Madras area in the southeastern portion of India, with the Gambians camped in the town of Karvetnagar. There was discussion about employing the division in the Allied invasion of Malaya, specifically at Kra, and consequently, some training was conducted with British Commandos in Madras. With Japanese fortunes on the decline and the 81 (WA) Division away from West Africa since July 1943, such plans were scrapped and the division was authorized to return home.[111] However, it would not be until December 1945 when the division left India for West Africa, with the Gambians returning to Bathurst in January 1946. After the cessation of hostilities against the Japanese, there was such a demand for shipping to repatriate large numbersof soldiers from Southeast Asia and elsewhere, that the West Africans of the 81 (WA) Division seemed to be of the lowest priority. Some historians argue, on slim evidence, that the slow repatriation of West Africans was actually a deliberate tactic of the British to eventually deploy the West Africans to Southeast Asian territories for postwar garrison duties, and ultimately ensure their delayed return to a volatile postwar political environment in West Africa.[112] Nonetheless, the 81 (WA) Division essentially sat idle at Madras for nine months waiting to return home, after it had just completed eighteen months of active service in Burma.[113]

Their time at Madras was largely banal for the West Africans. European officers and NCOs were given leave, and in fact, a large number of them returned home somehow finding transport that was not available for the rest of the division. However, the West Africans were barred from leave, except for a "leave camp" established on the coast. With such disparities in conditions and routine uneventful service, the West Africans were growing anxious.

In September, the division narrowly avoided a mutiny when companies of the Auxiliary Group demanded certain allowances owed to them and refused to go on parade. One company of 1 GR was called in to disperse the would-be mutineers without serious confrontation. Fortunately, it was an isolated incident, and the West Africans continued their stay in India without further problems. Regimental Sergeant Major (RSM) Samba Silla, a 25-year veteran of colonial military service, was instrumental in maintaining the overall discipline and composure of the Gambians during this anxious period. Silla dealt with complaints in an efficient manner and served as a valuable bridge between the officers and men in a period that posed very different problems than what 1 GR experienced during combat operations.[114] In fact, during his time in India awaiting repatriation, Silla became an imam and accommodated the Gambians' spiritual, as well as military, needs.[115]

Demobilization and slow repatriation were also serious problems for the rest of the Allied forces. For example, American forces in the Pacific were in a similar situation as the West Africans, largely being neglected because of extreme shipping demands across the globe, especially due to the repatriation of soldiers from the European theater.[116]

Before 1 GR returned to Bathurst on 8 January 1946, British officials in the Gambia initiated efforts to drastically reduce the military establishment in the colony.[118] On 15 July 1945, the commander of 2 GR stopped recruiting Gambians under emergency conditions stipulating service only for the duration of the war. However, the battalion continued to enlist soldiers willing to serve the usual six-year term. When 1 GR returned, 2 GR essentially dissolved and its members returned to civilian life with no reserve obligation. 1 GR remained as an entity until May 1946 when it was reduced to the strength of one company, which constituted a return to the military organization in the Gambia that had existed before the war.

After expansion to two battalions as necessitated by wartime conditions, the Gambia Company once again served as the only military establishment within the country. Along with this reduction, it also lost its regimental designation and institutional independence. Similar to the relationship that existed just before the war, the Gambia Company again formed part of the battalion-sized Sierra Leone Regiment (SLR) as "G" Company, under the command discretion of the Commanding Officer of the SLR. Unlike what happened after the First World War, however, British officials made substantial efforts to reenlist as many Burma veterans in the company ranks as possible to ensure the continuation of military competency and efficiency.[119] Furthermore, members of the Gambia Company accompanied the Royal West African Frontier Force contingent at the 1946 Victory Parade in London, a right denied to African soldiers after the

First World War.[120] Following 1918, British officials deliberately constructed the memory of a "white man's war" in celebrations and memorials, which marginalized African service in the war.[121] RWAFF attendance at the 1946 Victory Parade allowed West Africans a more prominent place within the official memory of the Second World War than what they received after the First World War.

Section Four Conclusion

THE SECOND WORLD WAR brought substantial changes to the Gambia Company and the Royal West African Frontier Force as a whole. In the face of the Vichy territorial threat in West Africa and Italian and German incursions elsewhere in Africa, the British rapidly expanded their colonial military forces in West Africa to unprecedented levels. The tiny Gambia boasted two infantry battalions and battalion strength support from the Gold Coast Regiment, the greatest level of military force ever achieved by the British in the Gambia. However, such expansion placed a disproportionate burden on the Gambian population compared to the rest of British West Africa; and as such, the Gambia provided more than its fair share to the defense of the greater British Empire.

That obligation of imperial defense sent the Gambians beyond Africa to one of the farthest reaches of the Empire to fight in a war that had little to do with the Gambia itself. Nonetheless, while in Burma the Gambians effectively supported Allied operations against the Japanese and added to the Gambia Company's storied reputation as a valuable military organization.

Conclusion

THE GAMBIA COMPANY CONTINUED as an attached unit of the Sierra Leone Regiment until 1950, when it reclaimed its institutional independence. After separation from the SLR, the Gambia Company was once again designated as the Gambia Regiment. However, this time, the Gambia Regiment's military culture and identity was officially celebrated and confirmed through the acquisition of Regimental Colours. The Gambia Company had been barred from receiving its own Colours in the 1920s on account of its small size.[1] In April 1950, the company sized Gambia Regiment finally received its Regimental Colours with eight battle honors:

Cameroon 1914-16
Nyangao
East Africa 1916-18
North Arakan
Kaladan
Mowdok
Myohaung
Burma 1943-45.

The Gambia Regiment received the Mowdok battle honor for its participation in Hubforce during the First Kaladan Campaign. No other Royal West African Frontier Force unit received this honor.[2] The action to grant Regimental Colours, although minor, was most likely informed by British attempts to strengthen ties with the Gambia during an era of increasing nationalist sentiments and calls for independence among Africans. Nonetheless, Regimental Colours represented official British acceptance of what the Gambia Company was during the entirety of its history—a uniquely Gambian military organization with regimental qualities.

Although the Gambia Regiment regained its independence from the SLR, it remained under the authority and administration of West Africa Command, and by extension the War Office. Since the Second World War, WAC remained in West Africa administering the RWAFF and support units, a task which, in the past fell under the respective colonial governments and the Colonial Office during peace time. For the Gambia, this arrangement was a blessing because it meant that the colonial government did not finance the Gambia Regiment, which allowed resources to be used elsewhere within the colony. However, WAC disbanded in 1956 and the War Office declared that it would no longer finance the Gambia Regiment after 1957, with the colonial government being forced to take up the financial burden of maintaining a military unit within its borders. Sir Percy Wyn-Harris, the Governor of the Gambia, decided that it was in the best interest of the colony to disband the Gambia Regiment and transfer its members to the Gambia Police. By March 1958, the Gambia Regiment was reduced to around 80 men, who, with the regiment's equipment, were fully absorbed into the Gambia Field Force, the paramilitary arm of the Gambia Police.[3] The Field Force was tasked to deal with civil unrest in Banjul and maintain order throughout the provinces during forthcoming elections.[4]

The decision to disband the Gambia Regiment had obvious financial incentives, but it was also related to the greater geopolitical considerations in the Senegambia region during the era of decolonization. British officials believed that the Gambia was too small and too vulnerable to function on its own as an independent country should it gain independence.

Therefore, the British hoped to pass the territory off to Senegal, which received independence from France in 1960. The discussion around this issue represented similar intentions as the British had held towards the Gambia during the colonial period when they intended to exchange the territory with the French. If the country were to be eventually absorbed by Senegal, then an independent military was unnecessary.[5]

Regardless of British intentions, the move was resisted by Gambian politicians, and the Gambia gained independence in 1965 and functioned for over 15 years without a military. Although the Gambia was not absorbed by Senegal, the two countries signed a mutual assistance pact which stipulated that Senegalese forces would aid the Gambia if required. In effect, the pact abolished the immediate need to create a Gambian military. In 1981, the pact was invoked when a failed coup attempt orchestrated by civilians and members of the Gambia Field Force required Senegalese military intervention. The coup attempt prompted the creation of the Gambia National Army (GNA). Elements of the Field Force merged with the GNA in 1985, which resulted in the creation of the Gambia Armed Forces (GAF), the military organization of the Gambia today.[6]

Although there is an indirect connection between the Gambia Company and the GAF through the Field Force, British military traditions and culture still persist in the Gambia. The GAF was set up and trained by British military advisors based on British military structures and facilitated by a common language. Furthermore, the Gambia and Britain often conduct joint training missions and maintain significant military partnerships. Ultimately, understanding the history of the Gambia Company exposes the foundations of martial culture and identity that persist in the Gambia today.[7]

Throughout its history, the Gambia Company was hampered by its small size relative to the greater WAFF/RWAFF. The company was initially founded under the mindset that its service in an unwanted territory was only temporary. However, after British realization that the Gambia would remain a British colony, substantial steps were made to nurture an efficient Gambian military organization. British officers stepped away from enlisting Sierra Leoneans and pursued policies that supported the development of an all-Gambian force. The British wanted to maintain an independent, locally recruited military organization in the Gambia, but at times this proved difficult to sustain. Often, the required number of Gambian recruits were hard to obtain, while the company sized establishment could not develop and train to the same level of military competency as larger military units. In effect, this forced the creation of a special relationship between the Gambia and Sierra Leone. Small numbers of Sierra Leoneans routinely travelled to Bathurst to enlist in the Gambia Company and, on several occasions, it was briefly attached to the Sierra Leone Battalion for training and imperial defense purposes. To some extent, there was also a special relationship with Senegal as many Senegalese soldiers enlisted within the Gambia Company.

Despite these difficulties, British officials continued in their attempts to maintain a distinct, independent military organization in the Gambia as a means to signal the Gambia's involvement in the greater British Empire. In reality, any RWAFF company could have garrisoned Bathurst to support the maintenance of British colonial authority in the Gambia. However, if a separate Gambian military organization served in the Gambia and participated in the RWAFF, even if only a company-sized unit, the Gambia could be seen as fulfilling its responsibilities as a member of the British Empire. Furthermore, the Gambia Company supported the British policy that each colonial governor maintained control of the colonial military forces within his territory for efficiency in responding to local events.

In effect, the British-led Gambia Company developed a military relationship between Bathurst and London to strengthen British colonialism in the Gambia and bolster the Gambia's perception of itself within the empire. Tasked to support this imperial vision were ordinary Gambian soldiers. Men like CSM Ebrima Jalu and RSM Samba Silla provided valuable service during demanding military operations and proved that African soldiers could function without the paternalistic guidance of their white officers. Within the colonial discourse, their service was a touchstone for British officials to argue that Gambians actively contributed to the "greater good" that the British Empire provided. Throughout this process, the service of Gambian soldiers within the Gambia Company contributed to the development of a Gambian military identity within the RWAFF.

The history of the Gambia Company is a story that should be more widely acknowledged. Gambian soldiers effectively supported the defense of the Gambia and the greater British Empire. They served with distinction during major military campaigns in Cameroon, East Africa, and Burma, but their story is often silenced because of the Gambia's small size and perceived insignificance. Of course, the Gambia did not, and could not, field a large colonial military organization like that of Nigeria or the Gold Coast (today's Ghana), but that should not detract from the service of Gambian soldiers. The Gambia Company overcame the limitations posed by its small size and independence to develop into and serve as an effective military organization.

Notes

Introduction

[1] David French, *Military Identities: The Regimental System, the British Army, and the British People, c.1870-2000*
(Oxford: Oxford University Press, 2005), 98.
[2] Benedict Anderson, *Imagined Communities: Reflections on the Origin and Spread of Nationalism* (London: Verso,1983), 7.
[3] The title of this book is borrowed from Lieutenant John Hamilton who served with the 1st Battalion Gambia Regiment during the Second World War and commented on the Gambia Company's regimental qualities. John Hamilton, *War Bush: 81 (West African) Division in Burma 1943-1945* (Norwich: Michael Russell Publishing Ltd,2001), 25.
[4] See the Nigerian soldier Isaac Fadoyebo's personal memoir featured prominently in Barnaby Phillips, *Another Man's War: The Story of a Burma Boy in Britain's Forgotten African Army* (London: Oneworld Publications, 2014).

Section One: The Origins and Formation of the Gambia Company

[1] A. Haywood and F. A. S. Clarke, *The History of the Royal West African Frontier Force* (Aldershot: Gale & PoldenLtd, 1964), 31-39. For detailed studies on the foundation of the WAFF also see Edho Ekoko, "The West African Frontier Force Revisited," *Journal of the Historical Society of Nigeria* 10, no. 1 (1979): 47–63 and S. C. Ukpabi, "The Origins of the West African Frontier Force," *Journal of the Historical Society of Nigeria* 3, no. 3 (1966): 485–501.
[2] J.M. Gray, *A History of the Gambia* (London: Frank Cass & Co, 1940), 9.
[3] Paul E. Lovejoy, *Transformations in Slavery: A History of Slavery in Africa*, 3rd ed (Cambridge: Cambridge University Press, 2011), 18-23. For more

information on the Trans-Atlantic Slave Trade also consult Jeremy Black, *The Atlantic Slave Trade in World History* (London: Routledge, 2015).

[4] Harry A. Gailey, *A History of the Gambia* (London: Routledge & Kegan Paul, 1964), 20-22.

[5] Gray, *A History of the Gambia*, 39-51.

[6] Gailey, *A History of the Gambia*, 23-25.

[7] Ibid., 25-33.

[8] Padraic X. Scanlan, *Freedom's Debtors: British Antislavery in Sierra Leone in the Age of Revolution* (New Haven: Yale University Press, 2017), 1-25. For more information on British abolitionism consult Derek R. Peterson, ed., *Abolitionism and Imperialism in Britain, Africa, and the Atlantic* (Athens, Ohio: Ohio University Press, 2010).

[9] Scanlan, *Freedom's Debtors*, 12.

[10] Arnold Hughes and David Perfect, *A Political History of The Gambia, 1816-1994* (Rochester: University of Rochester Press, 2006), 20.

[11] Gray, *A History of the Gambia*, 306-324.

[12] David E. Skinner, "Islam in Kombo: The Spiritual and Militant Jihād of Fodé Ibrahim Silla Turé," *Islamic Africa* 3, no. 1 (2012): 87–126.

[13] Hughes and Perfect, *A Political History of The Gambia, 1816-1994*, 13-26.

[14] Gray, *A History of the Gambia*, 388-398.

[15] For an in-depth study of Jihads in West Africa during this period consult Paul E. Lovejoy, *Jihād in West Africa during the Age of Revolutions* (Athens, Ohio: Ohio University Press, 2016).

[16] Hughes and Perfect, *A Political History of The Gambia, 1816-1994*, 42-43.

[17] Ibid., 42.

[18] Gray, *A History of the Gambia*, 388-391.

[19] Ibid., 302-303 and 366-367.

[20] For a discussion on the history of the slave trade in Africa and the transition to "Legitimate Commerce" consult Robin Law, ed., *From Slave Trade to "Legitimate" Commerce: The Commercial Transition in Nineteenth-Century West Africa* (Cambridge: Cambridge University Press, 1995) and Lovejoy, *Transformations in Slavery*.

[21] Gray, *A History of the Gambia*, 379-387.

[22] Hughes and Perfect, *A Political History of The Gambia, 1816-1994*, 68.

[23] Gailey, *A History of the Gambia*, 93.

[24] Hughes and Perfect, *A Political History of The Gambia, 1816-1994*, 43.

[25] Gailey, *A History of the Gambia*, 102.

[26] Hughes and Perfect, *A Political History of The Gambia, 1816-1994*, 72-73.

[27] Ibid., 6.

[28] Gailey, *A History of the Gambia*, 110.

[29] Richard Anderson, "The Diaspora of Sierra Leone's Liberated Africans: Enlistment, Forced Migration, and 'Liberation' at Freetown, 1808-1863," *African Economic History* 41, no. 1 (2013): 101–38.
[30] Scanlan, *Freedom's Debtors*, 22-23.
[31] For a detailed study on the WIR's formation and its history of military service within the West Indies consult Roger N. Buckley, *The British Army in the West Indies: Society and the Military in the Revolutionary Age* (Gainesville: University Press of Florida, 1998).
[32] Brian Dyde, *The Empty Sleeve: The Story of the West India Regiments of the British Army* (London: Hansib, 1997), 17-18.
[33] Roger N. Buckley, "The British Army's African Recruitment Policy, 1790-1807," *A Journal of African and Afro-American Studies* 5, Article 2 (2008): 1–12.
[34] Dyde, *The Empty Sleeve*, 23.
[35] Scanlan, *Freedom's Debtors*, 154-213.
[36] Dyde, *The Empty Sleeve*, 123-134.
[37] Dyde, *The Empty Sleeve*, 157-165.
[38] Gray, *A History of the Gambia*, 416-430.
[39] Gailey, *A History of the Gambia*, 60.
[40] Dyde, *The Empty Sleeve*, 215-224.
[41] The National Archives (UK) (hereafter NA), WO 106-6253, From Major Fairtlough, Royal Artillery, Commanding Troops, West Coast of Africa (Commanding Late Expedition to Gambia), to the Right Hon. The Secretary of State for War, War Office, London, 26 March 1894.
[42] H. Moyse-Bartlett, *The King's African Rifles: A Study in the Military History of East and Central Africa, 1890-1945* (England: Naval & Military Press, 1956), 43-48.
[43] Lt. Col. H. E. Brake, "Despatch from the Officer Commanding Gambia Field Force to the Right Honourable the Secretary of State for the Colonies," *The London Gazette*, September 10, 1901.
[44] Haywood and Clarke, *The History of the Royal West African Frontier Force*, 31-39.
[45] Siân Rees, *Sweet Water and Bitter: The Ships That Stopped the Slave Trade* (Durham, NH: University of New Hampshire Press, 2011), 5.
[46] Edho Ekoko, "The West African Frontier Force Revisited," 47–63.
[47] Ibid., 47.
[48] S. C. Ukpabi, "West Indian Troops and the Defense of British West Africa in the Nineteenth Century," *AfricanStudies Review* 17, no. 1 (1974): 133–50.
[49] Muriel Evelyn Chamberlain, *The Scramble for Africa* (New York: Routledge, 2013), 55-56.
[50] S. C. Ukpabi, "The Origins of the West African Frontier Force," 485–501.

[51] Ibid., 491.

[52] Marion Johnson, "The Slaves of Salaga," *The Journal of African History* 27, no. 2 (1986): 341–62.

[53] Haywood and Clarke, *The History of the Royal West African Frontier Force*, 40.

[54] Ukpabi, "The Origins of the West African Frontier Force," 495.

[55] Haywood and Clarke, *The History of the Royal West African Frontier Force*, 31-35.

[56] Ibid., 37.

[57] Ibid., 31-39.

[58] Andrew Stewart, "An Enduring Commitment: The British Military's Role in Sierra Leone," *Defence Studies* 8, no. 3 (September 1, 2008): 351–68.

[59] Edho Ekoko, "The Strategic-Imperial Factor in British Expansion in Sierra Leone, 1882-1899," *Journal of the Historical Society of Nigeria* 11, no. 1/2 (1981): 138–52.

[60] Anthony Clayton and David Killingray, *Khaki and Blue: Military and Police in British Colonial Africa* (Athens, Ohio: Ohio University Center for International Studies, 1989), 150-159.

[61] Heather Streets, *Martial Races: The Military, Race and Masculinity in British Imperial Culture, 1857-1914* (Manchester: Manchester University Press, 2004), 1. For more information on martial races in French colonial Africa consult Sarah Davis Westwood, "Ceɗɗo, Sòfa, Tirailleur: Slave Status and Military Identity in Nineteenth-Century Senegambia," *Slavery & Abolition* 39, no. 3 (July 3, 2018): 518–39 and Joe Lunn, "'Les Races Guerrierès':Racial Preconceptions in the French Military about West African Soldiers during the First World War," *Journal of Contemporary History* 34, no. 4 (1999): 517–36. Also, for a revisionist perspective that argues martial race ideologies were invented and advanced by Africans themselves, consult Myles Osborne, *Ethnicity and Empire in Kenya: Loyalty and Martial Race among the Kamba, c. 1800 to the Present* (New York, NY: Cambridge UniversityPress, 2014).

[62] Timothy Parsons, *The African Rank-and-File: Social Implications of Colonial Military Service in the King's African Rifles, 1902-1964* (Portsmouth, NH: Heinemann, 1999), 55.

[63] Timothy Stapleton, "Martial Identities in Colonial Nigeria (c.1900-1960)," *Journal of African Military History* 3,no. 1 (2019): 27.

[64] Ibid., 1-31.

[65] Parsons, *The African Rank-and-File*, 53. For information on martial race ideology in German colonial Africa and the socioeconomic influences behind askari service in the Schutztruppe consult Michelle Moyd, *Violent Intermediaries: African Soldiers, Conquest, and Everyday Colonialism in German East Africa* (Athens, Ohio: Ohio University Press, 2014).

[66] NA CO 445-34, Report of the Inspector General, WAFF on the Gambia Company, 1914.
[67] David Killingray, "The Idea of a British Imperial African Army," *The Journal of African History* 20, no. 3 (1979):421–36.
[68] Lunn, "'Les Races Guerrierès,'" 521.
[69] Myron Echenberg, *Colonial Conscripts: The Tirailleurs Sénégalais in French West Africa, 1857-1960* (Portsmouth, NH: Heinemann, 1991), 29.
[70] Ibid., 28-46. For more information on the Tirailleurs Senegalais consult Charles John Balesi, *From Adversaries toComrades-in-Arms: West Africans and the French Military, 1885-1918* (Waltham, Mass.: Crossroads Press, 1979); Joe Lunn, *Memoirs of the Maelstrom: A Senegalese Oral History of the First World War* (Portsmouth, NH: Heinemann, 1999); and Gregory Mann, *Native Sons: West African Veterans and France in the Twentieth Century* (Durham: Duke University Press, 2006).
[71] Killingray, "The Idea of a British Imperial African Army," 425.
[72] The Gambia Archives (hereafter GA), CSO 24-1, The Gambia Company History Book, Volume 1, 30 November 1901 to 7 December 1937.
[73] Parsons, *The African Rank-and-File*, 14-17. Other WAFF units had the luxury of enlisting soldiers from the already present constabularies and continuing recruiting practices in their respective regions. The Gambia Company did not have such a luxury.
[74] Haywood and Clarke, *The History of the Royal West African Frontier Force*, 40.
[75] GA CSO 24-1.
[76] NA CO 445-27, Minutes of the Report on Gambia Company WAFF, 1908.
[77] Gailey, *A History of the Gambia*, 110.
[78] NA CO 445-34, Report of the Inspector General, WAFF on the Gambia Company, 1914.
[79] NA CO 445-17, Report of the Inspector General, WAFF, on the Gambia Company, 1904.
[80] Brake, "Despatch from the Officer Commanding Gambia Field Force to the Right Honourable the Secretary ofState for the Colonies."
[81] Ekoko, "The West African Frontier Force Revisited," 56.
[82] GA CSO 24-1.
[83] NA CO 445-17, Report of the Inspector General, WAFF, on the Gambia Company, 1904.
[84] NA CO 445-27, Report of the Inspector General, WAFF, on the Gambia Company, 1908.
[85] David Killingray, "The 'Rod of Empire': The Debate over Corporal Punishment in the British African ColonialForces, 1888-1946," *The Journal of African History* 35, no. 2 (1994): 201–16.

[86] NA CO 445-17, Report of the Inspector General, WAFF, on the Gambia Company, 1904.
[87]David Killingray, "The Mutiny of the West African Regiment in the Gold Coast, 1901," *The International Journalof African Historical Studies* 16, no. 3 (1983): 441–54. For a labor perspective on mutinies in British colonial militaries consult Jama Mohamed, "The 1937 Somaliland Camel Corps Mutiny: A Contrapuntal Reading," *The International Journal of African Historical Studies* 33, no. 3 (2000): 615–34. For information on mutiny trends and common grievances among modern African soldiers, which overlap with African soldiers of the colonial period, consult Maggie Dwyer, *Soldiers in Revolt: Army Mutinies in Africa* (Oxford: Oxford University Press, 2017).
[88] GA CSO 24-1.
[89] Ukpabi, "West Indian Troops and the Defense of British West Africa in the Nineteenth Century," 149.
[90] NA CO 445-17, Annual Report Gambia Company WAFF, 1903.
[91] NA CO 445-17, Report of the Inspector General, WAFF, on the Gambia Company, 1904.
[92] NA CO 445-17.
[93] NA CO 445-22, Annual Report Gambia Company WAFF, 1905.
[94] NA CO 445-22.
[95] N. J. Miners, *The Nigerian Army 1956-1966* (London: Methuen, 1971), 20-22.
[96] NA CO 445-22.
[97] GA CSO 3-3, Report of the Inspector General, WAFF, on the Gambia Company, 1906.
[98] NA CO 445-27, Minutes of the Report on the Gambia Company, 1908.
[99] NA CO 445-27, From Acting Governor of the Gambia to the Secretary of State for the Colonies, 20 October 1908.
[100] Killingray, "The Mutiny of the West African Regiment in the Gold Coast, 1901," 441-454.
[101] Clayton and Killingray, *Khaki and Blue*, 182.
[102] NA CO 445-27, Minutes of the Report on the Gambia Company, 1908.
[103] GA CSO 3-3, Minutes of the Report on the Gambia Company, 1906.
[104] NA CO 445-27, Report of the Inspector General, WAFF, on the Gambia Company, 1908.
[105] NA CO 445-27.
[106] Echenberg, *Colonial Conscripts*, 14.
[107] NA CO 820-1-3, Report of the Inspector General, WAFF, on the Gambia Company, 1926.
[108] Parsons, *The African Rank-and-File*, 53.

[109] Hughes and Perfect, *A Political History of The Gambia, 1816-1994*, 18.
[110] NA CO 445-34.
[111] NA CO 820-4-6, Inspection Report on the Gambia Company, WAFF, 1927-1928.
[112] Ekoko, "The West African Frontier Force Revisited," 57-59.
[113] NA CO 445-32, Report of the Inspector General, WAFF, on the Gambia Company, 1912.
[114] NA CO 445-17, Annual Report Gambia Company, 1903.
[115] NA CO 445-17, Report of the Inspector General, WAFF, on the Gambia Company, 1904 and NA CO 445-34.
[116] NA CO 445-30, Report of the Inspector General, WAFF, on the Gambia Company, 1910.
[117] NA CO 445-34.
[118] GA CSO 24-1.
[119] NA CO 445-32.
[120] NA CO 445-33, Minutes on Gambia Company Increase, 1913.
[121] NA CO 445-34.

Section Two: The Gambia Company during the First World War, 1914-1918

[1] Hew Strachan, *The First World War in Africa* (Oxford: Oxford University Press, 2004), 184. This source offersthe most complete overview of the First World War in Africa. See also Byron Farwell, *The Great War in Africa* (New York: W.W. Norton & Company, 1986); Melvin Page, ed., *Africa and the First World War* (New York: Palgrave Macmillan, 1987); and Edward Paice, *Tip and Run: The Untold Tragedy of the Great War in Africa* (London: Weidenfeld & Nicolson, 2007).
[2] For a detailed study of the social history of the *Schutztruppe* in German East Africa consult Moyd, *Violent Intermediaries* and Michelle Moyd, "Centring a Sideshow: Local Experiences of the First World War in Africa,"*First World War Studies* 7, no. 2 (May 3, 2016): 111–30.
[3] P. H. S. Hatton, "The Gambia, the Colonial Office, and the Opening Months of the First World War," *The Journal of African History* 7, no. 1 (1966): 123–31.
[4] E. Howard Gorges, *The Great War in West Africa* (East Sussex: The Naval & Military Press, 1916), 60-81.
[5] Strachan, *The First World War in Africa*, 106.
[6] Hatton, "The Gambia, the Colonial Office, and the Opening Months of the First World War," 125.
[7] NA CO 445-34, WAFF Despatches, 1914.
[8] NA CO 445-33, Governor Gallway to Hon. Colonial Secretary, 19 July 1913.
[9] GA CSO 24-1, The Gambia Company History Book, Volume 1, 30 November

1901 to 7 December 1937.

[10] NA WO-95-5388-4, Cameroons – Gambia Company WAFF.

[11] Strachan, *The First World War in Africa*, 13-18.

[12] F. J. Moberly, *Military Operations, Togoland and the Cameroons* (London: Imperial War Museum, Dept. of Printed Books, 1931), *1914-1916*, 50.

[13] Strachan, *The First World War in Africa*, 31.

[14] GA CSO 24-1.

[15] Strachan, *The First World War in Africa*, 30.

[16] Gorges, *The Great War in West Africa*, 90.

[17] Strachan, *The First World War in Africa*, 21.

[18] Ibid., 19.

[19] Ibid., 21-29.

[20] George Njung, "Soldiers of Their Own: Honor, Violence, Resistance and Conscription in Colonial Cameroon during the First World War" (PhD Dissertation, University of Michigan, 2016), 116-130.

[21] Moberly, *Military Operations, Togoland and the Cameroons, 1914-1916*, 55-97.

[22] Ibid., 58-112.

[23] Haywood and Clarke, *The History of the Royal West African Frontier Force*, 121.

[24] Moberly, *Military Operations, Togoland and the Cameroons, 1914-1916*, 114-119.

[25] Ibid., 69-72.

[26] Haywood and Clarke, *The History of the Royal West African Frontier Force*, 121.

[27] Moberly, *Military Operations, Togoland and the Cameroons, 1914-1916*, 78-125.

[28] Ibid., 126-131.

[29] GA CSO 24-1.

[30] Moberly, *Military Operations, Togoland and the Cameroons, 1914-1916*, 123.

[31] Haywood and Clarke, *The History of the Royal West African Frontier Force*, 305.

[32] Moberly, *Military Operations, Togoland and the Cameroons, 1914-1916*, 145.

[33] Ibid., 141-144.

[34] Haywood and Clarke, *The History of the Royal West African Frontier Force*, 134-139.

[35] Moberly, *Military Operations, Togoland and the Cameroons, 1914-1916*, 158-170.

[36] GA CSO 24-1.

[37] Moberly, *Military Operations, Togoland and the Cameroons*, 1914-1916, 213-

216.
[38] NA WO-95-5388-4.
[39] Strachan, *The First World War in Africa*, 24.
[40] GA CSO 24-1.
[41] NA WO-95-5388-4.
[42] Moberly, *Military Operations, Togoland and the Cameroons, 1914-1916*, 255-260.
[43] Ibid., 256.
[44] Haywood and Clarke, *The History of the Royal West African Frontier Force*, 147-148.
[45] GA CSO 24-1.
[46] "Award for Bravery," *African Mail*, January 21, 1916, 164.
[47] GA CSO 24-1.
[48] GA CSO 24-1.
[49] Moberly, *Military Operations, Togoland and the Cameroons, 1914-1916*, 277-288.
[50] Strachan, *The First World War in Africa*, 44.
[51] Haywood and Clarke, *The History of the Royal West African Frontier Force*, 150.
[52] Moberly, *Military Operations, Togoland and the Cameroons, 1914-1916*, 285-317.
[53] GA CSO 24-1.
[54] Moberly, *Military Operations, Togoland and the Cameroons, 1914-1916*, 320-328.
[55] Haywood and Clarke, *The History of the Royal West African Frontier Force*, 155.
[56] Moberly, *Military Operations, Togoland and the Cameroons, 1914-1916*, 328-334.
[57] GA CSO 24-1.
[58] Haywood and Clarke, *The History of the Royal West African Frontier Force*, 165.
[59] Ibid., 165.
[60] GA CSO 24-1.
[61] GA CSO 24-1.
[62] Strachan, *The First World War in Africa*, 56-60.
[63] Moberly, *Military Operations, Togoland and the Cameroons, 1914-1916*, 376.
[64] Strachan, *The First World War in Africa*, 54-55.
[65] Ibid., 57.
[66] Ibid., 57-58.
[67] Njung, "Soldiers of Their Own," 337-377.
[68] GA CSO 24-1.

[69] NA CO 445-36, Captain Stanford-Samuel to Hon. Colonial Secretary, 16 June 1916.

[70] Festus Cole, "Sierra Leone and World War 1" (PhD Dissertation, London, University of London - School of Oriental and African Studies, 1994), 65-67.

[71] NA CO 445-35, The Gambia Company Recruiting Report, 1915.

[72] NA CO 445-35.

[73] GA CSO 24-1.

[74] Harold E. Raugh, *The Victorians at War, 1815-1914: An Encyclopedia of British Military History* (Santa Barbara: ABC-CLIO, 2004), 182. See also Spencer Jones, *From Boer War to World War: Tactical Reform of the British Army, 1902-1914* (Norman: University of Oklahoma Press, 2012).

[75] Haywood and Clarke, *The History of the Royal West African Frontier Force*, 49.

[76] Aimée Fox-Godden, "Beyond the Western Front: The Practice of Inter-Theatre Learning in the British Army during the First World War," *War in History* 23, no. 2 (2016): 190–209.

[77] NA CO 445-37, Captain Thurston to Captain Beattie, 22 July 1916.

[78] NA CO 445-36, Captain Thurston to Captain Beattie, 22 July 1916.

[79] GA CSO 24-1.

[80] Echenberg, *Colonial Conscripts*, 26-27.

[81] For more information on British West African carriers and carriers in the East Africa Campaign consult DavidKillingray and James Matthews, "Beasts of Burden: British West African Carriers in the First World War," *Canadian Journal of African Studies / Revue Canadienne Des Études Africaines* 13, no. 1/2 (1979): 5–23 and Geoffrey Hodges, *The Carrier Corps: Military Labor in the East African Campaign, 1914-1918* (New York: Greenwood Press, 1986).

[82] Echenberg, *Colonial Conscripts*, 27-71.

[83] GA CSO 3-26, Colonial Secretary to all the Traveling Commissioners, 3 November 1918.

[84] GA CSO 3-26, Immigration of Natives from French Territories to Escape Military Service, 1916.

[85] NA CO 445-36, Captain Stanford-Samuel to Colonial Secretary Bonar Law, 16 June 1916.

[86] NA CO 445-36, Thurston to Beattie.

[87] NA CO 445-36, Secretary Bonar Law – Signed Minutes, 4 August 1916.

[88] Haywood and Clarke, *The History of the Royal West African Frontier Force*, 176-178.

[89] Tim Stapleton, "The Africanization of British Imperial Forces in the East African Campaign," in *Turning Point 1917: The British Empire at War*, ed. Douglas Delaney and Nikolas Gardner (Vancouver: UBC Press, 2017), 136-149.

[90] GA CSO 3-28A, Secretary Bonar Law to Governor Cameron, 8 December 1916.
[91] NA CO 445-55, Governor Armitage to the Colonial Secretary, 11 February 1921.
[92] Cole, "Sierra Leone and World War 1," 65-107.
[93] NA CO 445-38.
[94] GA CSO 24-1.
[95] NA CO 445-38, Captain Law to Acting Colonial Secretary, 8 March 1917.
[96] NA CO 445-38.
[97] NA CO 445-38, Governor Edward Cameron to Secretary of State for the Colonies, 10 June 1917.
[98] NA CO 445-38, Governor Edward Cameron to all Head Chiefs, 24 April 1917.
[99] NA CO 445-43, Account of the Gambia Company in East Africa, 31 May 1918.
[100] NA CO 445-38, Governor Edward Cameron to Colonel A. Haywood, 12 March 1917.
[101] Strachan, *The First World War in Africa*, 101.
[102] Ibid., 101-102. Also consult Paul Emil von Lettow-Vorbeck, *My Reminiscences of East Africa* (Ravenio Books,1920) and Charles Hordern, *Military Operations: East Africa* (London: H.M. Stationery Office, 1941).
[103] Ross Anderson, *The Forgotten Front: The East African Campaign, 1914 -1918* (The History Press, 2014), 37.
[104] Stapleton, "The Africanization of British Imperial Forces in the East African Campaign," 138-139. See also Ross Anderson, *The Battle of Tanga 1914* (Charleston: Tempus Publishing Inc., 2002).
[105] Anderson, *The Forgotten Front,* 59-62.
[106] Anderson, *The Forgotten Front*, 12-13.
[107] Strachan, *The First World War in Africa*, 95.
[108] Stapleton, "The Africanization of British Imperial Forces in the East African Campaign," 153-154.
[109] Strachan, *The First World War in Africa*, 126.
[110] Stapleton, "The Africanization of British Imperial Forces in the East African Campaign," 140.
[111] Anderson, *The Forgotten Front*, 130-133.
[112] Stapleton, "The Africanization of British Imperial Forces in the East African Campaign," 150-151.
[113] Strachan, *The First World War in Africa*, 131-164.
[114] W. D. Downes, *With the Nigerians in East Africa* (London: Methuen & Co, 1919), 294.
[115] NA CO 445-43.

[116] NA WO-95-5347-11, War Diary of the Gambia Company attached Nigeria Contingent, 1917.
[117] Hodges, *The Carrier Corps*, 110-111. Also consult Donald C. Savage and J. Forbes Munro, "Carrier Corps Recruitment in the British East Africa Protectorate 1914-1918," *The Journal of African History* 7, no. 2 (1966):313–42.
[118] NA WO-95-5347-11.
[119] NA CO 445-43.
[120] NA WO-95-5347-11.
[121] NA WO-95-5347-11.
[122] Stapleton, "The Africanization of British Imperial Forces in the East African Campaign," 148.
[123] Anderson, *The Forgotten Front*, 287-296.
[124] NA WO-95-5347-11.
[125] NA WO-95-5347-11.
[126] Downes, *With the Nigerians in East Africa*, 209-225.
[127] NA CO 445-43.
[128] NA WO-95-5347-11.
[129] NA CO 445-43.
[130] NA WO-95-5347-11.
[131] NA CO 445-43.
[132] Haywood and Clarke, *The History of the Royal West African Frontier Force*, 234-235.
[133] NA CO 445-43.
[134] Anderson, *The Forgotten Front*, 301.
[135] Strachan, *The First World War in Africa*, 181-172.
[136] NA WO-95-5347-11.
[137] NA CO 445-43.
[138] NA CO 445-43.
[139] NA CO 445-43.
[140] Haywood and Clarke, *The History of the Royal West African Frontier Force*, 241.
[141] GA CSO 24-1.
[142] Haywood and Clarke, *The History of the Royal West African Frontier Force*, 252.
[143] NA CO 445-36.
[144] Gregory Maddox, "Mtunya: Famine in Central Tanzania, 1917-20," *The Journal of African History* 31, no. 2(1990): 181–97.
[145] Strachan, *The First World War in Africa*, 10.

Section Three: The Gambia Company during the Interwar Period, 1918-1939

[1] David French, *Raising Churchill's Army: The British Army and the War Against Germany 1919-1945* (Oxford: Oxford University Press, 2000), 13-15.
[2] Haywood and Clarke, *The History of the Royal West African Frontier Force*, 320.
[3] David E. Omissi, *Air Power and Colonial Control: The Royal Air Force 1919-1939* (Manchester: Manchester University Press, 1990), 211.
[4] Clayton and Killingray, *Khaki and Blue*, 164.
[5] Barbara Bush, *Imperialism, Race, and Resistance: Africa and Britain, 1919-1945* (London: Routledge, 1999), 20.
[6] Martin Thomas, *Violence and Colonial Order: Police, Workers and Protest in the European Colonial Empires, 1918-1940* (Cambridge: Cambridge University Press, 2012), 8.
[7] NA CO 445-45, Secretary of State for the Colonies to the Governor of the Gambia, 5 June 1918.
[8] NA CO 445-45. Haywood and Clarke, *The History of the Royal West African Frontier Force*, 252.
[9] Killingray, "The Idea of a British Imperial African Army," 421–36.
[10] NA CO 445-43, Minutes on the State's Views as to Proposed Stoppage of Recruiting, 5 March 1918.
[11] NA CO 445-43, Governor Edward Cameron to the Secretary of State for the Colonies, 5 March 1918.
[12] NA CO 445-43.
[13] NA CO 445-55, Report of the Inspector General, WAFF, on the Gambia Company, 1921.
[14] GA CSO 24-1, The Gambia Company History Book, Volume 1, 30 November 1901 to 7 December 1937.
[15] NA CO 445-50, The Officer Commanding, the Gambia Company WAFF to Colonial Secretary, Bathurst, 7February 1920.
[16] NA CO 445-62, Report of the Inspector General, WAFF, on the Gambia Company, January 1923.
[17] NA CO 445-62, Report of the Training of Reserves for 1923.
[18] NA CO 445-64, Governor Armitage to the Secretary of State for the Colonies, 12 March 1924.
[19] NA CO 445-62, Report of the Inspector General, WAFF, on the Gambia Company, January 1923.
[20] NA CO 445-55.
[21] NA CO 445-62.
[22] NA CO 445-68, Annual Report on the Gambia Company, WAFF, 21 December 1925.

[23] NA CO 445-55.
[24] NA CO 445-64, J.H. Thomas to Governor Armitage, 2 June 1924.
[25] NA CO 445-64.
[26] Haywood and Clarke, *The History of the Royal West African Frontier Force*, 320.
[27] NA CO 445-64, Governor Armitage to the Secretary of State for the Colonies, 8 September 1924.
[28] NA CO 445-64, Minutes on the Situation of Armed Police Force for the Gambia Company, 3 October 1924.
[29] NA CO 445-68.
[30] NA CO 820-7-8, Minutes Regarding the Abolition of the Gambia Company, 1 February 1929.
[31] NA CO 820-12-3, Minutes Regarding the Inspection Report on the Gambia Company, 21 April 1931.
[32] Clayton and Killingray, *Khaki and Blue*, 150-159.
[33] NA CO 445-64, Annual Report on the Gambia Company, WAFF, 31 December 1923.
[34] NA CO 820-19-10, Inspector General's Report of the Gambia Company, RWAFF, 1935.
[35] NA CO 445-67, Acting Governor to the Secretary of State for the Colonies, 19 August 1925.
[36] NA CO 445-67, Annual Report on the Gambia Company, WAFF, 31 December 1924.
[37] NA CO 537-954, Report on the Combatant Manpower Native Races of British West Africa, 4 July 1923.
[38] NA CO 820-1-3, Governor Armitage to the Secretary of State for the Colonies, 23 December 1926.
[39] Clayton and Killingray, *Khaki and Blue*, 179.
[40] NA CO 820-1-3, Colonel S.S. Butler to the Secretary of State for the Colonies, 22 November 1926.
[41] NA CO 820-4-6, Inspection Report on the Gambia Company, WAFF, 1927-1928.
[42] Stapleton, "Martial Identities in Colonial Nigeria (c.1900-1960)," 1–32.
[43] William Pratt, "Medicine and Obedience: Canadian Army Morale, Discipline and Surveillance in the Second World War, 1939-1945" (PhD Dissertation, Calgary, University of Calgary, 2015), 240-273.
[44] Mark Harrison, "The British Army and the Problem of Venereal Disease in France and Egypt during the First World War," *Medical History* 39, no. 2 (1995): 133–158.
[45] Mark Harrison, "Medicine and the Culture of Command: The Case of Malaria Control in the British Army during the Two World Wars," *Medical History* 40,

no. 4 (1996): 437–452.
[46] NA CO 445-67.
[47] NA CO 820-34-9, Inspector General Report on the Sierra Leone Battalion and the Gambia Company, WAFF, 21 March 1939.
[48] Arnold Hughes and David Perfect, "Trade Unionism in the Gambia," *African Affairs* 88, no. 353 (1989): 549–72.
[49] GA CSO 24-1.
[50] The Gambia Company moved its headquarters to Cape St. Mary and was permanently garrisoned there since April 1922. NA CO 445-64.
[51] GA CSO 24-1.
[52] Hughes and Perfect, "Trade Unionism in the Gambia," 549-572.
[53] GA CSO 24-1.
[54] NA CO 537-954.
[55] GA CSO 24-1.
[56] NA CO 820-34-9.
[57] GA CSO 24-1.
[58] Haywood and Clarke, *The History of the Royal West African Frontier Force*, 324-327.
[59] NA CO 820-35-6, Acting Governor of Sierra Leone to the Governor of the Gambia, 14 January 1939.
[60] GA CSO 24-4, Gambia Company History Book, Volume II, Commenced 1 January 1938.
[61] NA CO 820-35-6, The Officer Commanding, the Gambia Company, RWAFF to the Honourable Colonial Secretary, Bathurst, 20 December 1938.
[62] NA CO 820-35-6, The Officer Commanding Sierra Leone Battalion, RWAFF, to the Honourable Colonial Secretary, Freetown, 28 December 1938.
[63] NA CO 820-35-6.
[64] NA CO 820-34-9, Governor Southorn to Colonial Office, 26 July 1939.
[65] LaRay Denzer, "Wallace-Johnson and the Sierra Leone Labor Crisis of 1939," *African Studies Review* 25, no. 2/3(1982): 159–83.
[66] GA CSO 24-4.
[67] Bush, *Imperialism, Race, and Resistance*, 117-119.
[68] Festus Cole, "Defining the 'Flesh' of the Black Soldier in Colonial Sierra Leone: Background to the Gunners' Mutiny of 1939," *Canadian Journal of African Studies / Revue Canadienne Des Études Africaines* 48, no. 2 (May 4, 2014): 275–95.
[69] NA CO 820-34-9, Inspector General Report on the Sierra Leone Battalion and the Gambia Company, WAFF, 21March 1939.
[70] NA CO 820-30-2, Annual Report on the Gambia Company, RWAFF, 28

February 1938.
[71] NA CO 820-34-9.
[72] NA CO 820-34-9, Minutes Regarding the Defense Considerations of the Gambia, 31 May 1939.
[73] NA CO 820-34-9, Minutes.
[74] NA CO 820-34-9, Inspector General Report on the Sierra Leone Battalion and the Gambia Company, WAFF, 21 March 1939.

Section Four: The Gambia "Company" during the Second World War, 1939-1945

[1] Andrew Stewart, *The First Victory: The Second World War and the East Africa Campaign* (New Haven: Yale University Press, 2016), 48-70.
[2] Ashley Jackson, *The British Empire and the Second World War* (London: Hambledon Continuum, 2006), 171.
[3] David Killingray and Richard Rathbone, eds., *Africa and the Second World War* (New York: Palgrave Macmillan, 1986), 1-17. Also consult David Killingray, *Fighting for Britain: African Soldiers in the Second World War* (Woodbridge: Boydell & Brewer Ltd, 2010) and Judith Byfield et al., eds., *Africa and World War II* (New York: Cambridge University Press, 2015).
[4] Eric T. Jennings, *Free French Africa in World War II: The African Resistance* (New York: Cambridge University Press, 2015), 1-49.
[5] Ruth Ginio, *French Colonialism Unmasked: The Vichy Years in French West Africa* (Lincoln: University of Nebraska Press, 2006), 1.
[6] Ibid., 4-9.
[7] Judith Byfield, "Producing for the War," in *Africa and World War II*, ed. Judith Byfield et al., 24-43.
[8] John Williams, *The Guns of Dakar: September 1940* (London: Heinemann, 1976), 164-184.
[9] Jennings, *Free French Africa in World War II*, 111-140.
[10] Nancy Ellen Lawler, *Soldiers, Airmen, Spies, and Whisperers: The Gold Coast in World War II* (Athens, Ohio:Ohio University Press, 2002), 1-38.
[11] GA CSO 4-85, Memorandum for the General Officer Commanding the British Forces in West Africa and His Subordinate Commanders, July 1940.
[12] Haywood and Clarke, *The History of the Royal West African Frontier Force*, 328-361.
[13] GA CSO 24-4, Gambia Company History Book, Volume II, Commenced 1 January 1938.
[14] NA CO 820-34-9, Inspector General Report on the Sierra Leone Battalion and the Gambia Company, WAFF, 21 March 1939.

[15] Stewart, "An Enduring Commitment," 351–368.
[16] GA CSO 4-64, Commissioner of the South Bank Province to the Honourable Acting Colonial Secretary at Bathurst, 24 January 1941.
[17] The Oxford Records Development Project, Weston Library, Oxford (hereafter ORDP) Memoirs of Lieutenant J.A.L. Hamilton, 29 December 1981.
[18] GA CSO 4-116, Acting Governor, Gambia to G.O.C. West Africa, 21 October 1940.
[19] GA CSO 4-64, Headquarters Gambia Area to the Honourable Colonial Secretary, Bathurst, 15 March 1941.
[20] Jackson, *The British Empire and the Second World War*, 183-186.
[21] ORDP, Memoirs of Major N.D. Poulsen.
[22] GA CSO 4-64.
[23] GA CSO 4-64, Acting Colonial Secretary, Bathurst to the Deputy Chairman, West African Governors' Conference, 16 March 1941.
[24] David Killingray, "Labour Mobilisation in British Colonial Africa for the War Effort, 1939-46," in *Africa and the Second World War*, 68–96.
[25] GA CSO 4-64.
[26] Bonny Ibhawoh, "Second World War Propoganda, Imperial Idealism and Anti-Colonial Nationalism in British West Africa," *Nordic Journal of African Studies* 16, no. 2 (2007): 221–43.
[27] Echenberg, *Colonial Conscripts*, 30.
[28] GA CSO 4-64.
[29] GA CSO 4-64, Labour Advisor to the Honourable Secretary of State for the Colonies, 20 April 1940.
[30] GA CSO 4-64, Report on the Manpower Statistics of British West Africa, 10 March 1941.
[31] GA CSO 4-65, Manpower Requirements of the Army, 3 October 1942.
[32] ORDP, Hamilton.
[33] GA CSO 4-67, Minutes Regarding Military Recruiting in the Gambia, 31 August 1944.
[34] GA CSO 4-66, Recruitment of French Africans in the West African Forces, 4 July 1944.
[35] Clayton and Killingray, *Khaki and Blue*, 160-162.
[36] Czeslaw Jesman, "The Polish Experiment in West Africa During World War II," *Instituto Italiano per l'Africa el'Oriente* 20, no. 4 (1965): 413–26.
[37] ORDP, Memoirs of Major T.A. Kennedy-Davis.
[38] Timothy Stapleton, *No Insignificant Part: the Rhodesia Native Regiment and the East Africa Campaign of the First World War* (Waterloo, Ont.: Wilfrid Laurier University Press, 2006), 144.
[39] ORDP, Poulsen.

[40] GA CSO 3-392, Report on the Disturbances at Brikama, 24 December 1941.
[41] GA CSO 3-393 Military Relations in the South Bank Province. GA CSO 3-415, Military Relations in the North Bank Province.
[42] GA CSO 3-394, Disturbance at Brikama, Destruction of Police Lines by Military.
[43] Timothy Stapleton, "Barracks Islam and Command Christianity: Religion in Britain's West African Colonial Army (c.1900–1960)," *War & Society* 39, no. 1 (January 2, 2020): 1–22.
[44] Robert E. Handloff, "Prayers, Amulets, and Charms: Health and Social Control," *African Studies Review* 25, no. 2/3 (1982): 185–94; David Owusu-Ansah, "Prayer, Amulets, and Healing," in *The History of Islam in Africa*, ed. N. Levtzion and R. Pouwels (Athens: Ohio University Press, 2000); David Owusu-Ansah, "Islamic Influence in a Forest Kingdom: The Role of Protective Amulets in Early 19th Century Asante," *Transafrican Journal of History* 12 (1983): 100–133.
[45] Haywood and Clarke, *The History of the Royal West African Frontier Force*, 373.
[46] ORDP, Poulsen.
[47] Killingray, "The Idea of a British Imperial African Army," 421–36.
[48] Haywood and Clarke, *The History of the Royal West African Frontier Force*, 506.
[49] ORDP, Poulsen.
[50] ORDP, Memoirs of Lieutenant Colonel J.R. Filmer-Bennett.
[51] ORDP, Hamilton.
[52] GA CSO 4-67.
[53] Frank McLynn, *The Burma Campaign: Disaster into Triumph 1942-45* (New Haven: Yale University Press, 2010), 1-16.
[54] William Slim, *Defeat into Victory* (London: Cassell & Co Ltd., 1956), 147-166.
[55] Ibid, 128-146.
[56] Phillips, *Another Man's War*, 302-315.
[57] Slim, *Defeat into Victory*, 151.
[58] Haywood and Clarke, *The History of the Royal West African Frontier Force*, 382.
[59] ORDP, Hamilton, Report from Major General Woolner to GOC West Africa, July 1944.
[60] ORDP, Hamilton, Report from Major General Woolner to GOC West Africa, July 1944.
[61] John Igbino, *Spidermen: Nigerian Chindits and Wingate's Operation Thursday Burma 1943-1944* (Bloomington, IN: Author House, 2018), 19-22.
[62] Hamilton, *War Bush: 81 (West African) Division in Burma 1943-1945*, 43-50.

[63] ORDP, Hamilton, Report from Major General Woolner to GOC West Africa, July 1944.
[64] Michael Pearson, *The Burma Air Campaign, 1941-1945* (South Yorkshire: Pen & Sword Books Ltd., 2006), 104-105.
[65] Haywood and Clarke, *The History of the Royal West African Frontier Force*, 470.
[66] Hamilton, *War Bush: 81 (West African) Division in Burma 1943-1945*, 323-329.
[67] Slim, *Defeat into Victory*, 122-123.
[68] Mark Harrison, *Medicine and Victory: British Military Medicine in the Second World War* (Oxford: Oxford University Press, 2004), 201-211.
[69] ORDP, Hamilton.
[70] ORDP, Poulsen.
[71] Hamilton, *War Bush: 81 (West African) Division in Burma 1943-1945*, 53-65.
[72] Ibid., 73-80.
[73] ORDP, Hamilton, Report from Major General Woolner to GOC West Africa, July 1944.
[74] Hamilton, *War Bush: 81 (West African) Division in Burma 1943-1945*, 94.
[75] Haywood and Clarke, *The History of the Royal West African Frontier Force*, 391.
[76] Phillips, *Another Man's War*, 144-147.
[77] ORDP, Memoir of Lieutenant Colonel George Laing.
[78] ORDP, Laing.
[79] ORDP, Hamilton.
[80] ORDP, Hamilton.
[81] ORDP, Hamilton.
[82] Hamilton, *War Bush: 81 (West African) Division in Burma 1943-1945*, 116-122.
[83] Haywood and Clarke, *The History of the Royal West African Frontier Force*, 394-401.
[84] ORDP, Laing.
[85] Hamilton, *War Bush: 81 (West African) Division in Burma 1943-1945*, 165-166.
[86] Haywood and Clarke, *The History of the Royal West African Frontier Force*, 406-407.
[87] NA WO-373-35-285.
[88] NA WO-373-36-382, Award Citation for Private Musa N'Jie, 18 October 1944.
[89] NA WO-373-35-382, Award Citation for Private Bokari Bojan, 30 May 1944.

[90] ORDP, Poulsen.
[91] ORDP, Poulsen.
[92] Hamilton, *War Bush: 81 (West African) Division in Burma 1943-1945*, 173-181.
[93] Ibid., 181-185.
[94] Haywood and Clarke, *The History of the Royal West African Frontier Force*, 429-430.
[95] Ibid., 433-435.
[96] NA WO-373-36-378, Award Citation for Lance Corporal Samba Jallow, 19 November 1944.
[97] NA WO-373-36-379, Award Citation for Lance Corporal Yaryah Jallow, 7 December 1944 and NA WO-373-36-214, Award Citation for Captain Jan Zieleznik, 7 December 1944.
[98] Hamilton, *War Bush: 81 (West African) Division in Burma 1943-1945*, 206-232.
[99] Ibid., 233.
[100] NA WO-373-36-380, Award Citation for Private Kinti Kamara, 27 December 1944.
[101] Hamilton, *War Bush: 81 (West African) Division in Burma 1943-1945*, 233-236.
[102] Ibid., 243.
[103] NA WO-373-36-381, Award Citation for Private Dudu N'Dowe, 11 January 1945.
[104] Hamilton, *War Bush: 81 (West African) Division in Burma 1943-1945*, 252-253.
[105] Phillips O'Brien, *How the War was Won: Air-Sea Power and Allied Victory in World War II* (Cambridge: Cambridge University Press, 2015), 412-429.
[106] McLynn, *The Burma Campaign*, 420-434.
[107] Haywood and Clarke, *The History of the Royal West African Frontier Force*, 449.
[108] Ibid., 450-451.
[109] McLynn, *The Burma Campaign: Disaster*, 433.
[110] Hamilton, *War Bush: 81 (West African) Division in Burma 1943-1945*, 195.
[111] Haywood and Clarke, *The History of the Royal West African Frontier Force*, 432.
[112] Emmanuel Nwafor Mordi, "'No Longer Required for Operations': Troops' Repatriation to West Africa after the Second World War, 1945–1950," *The Journal of Imperial and Commonwealth History*, June 9, 2020, 1–30.
[113] ORDP, Hamilton.
[114] NA WO-373-82-444, Award Citation for Regimental Sergeant Major

Samba Silla, 12 September 1945.

[115] Stapleton, "Barracks Islam and Command Christianity: Religion in Britain's West African Colonial Army(c.1900–1960)," 19.

[116] R. Alton Lee, "The Army 'Mutiny' of 1946," *The Journal of American History* 53, no. 3 (1966): 555–71.

[117] Hamilton, *War Bush: 81 (West African) Division in Burma 1943-1945*, 317-320.

[118] *RWAFF News*, "First Contingent of Gambian Troops Arrive, Bathurst Welcomes Soldiers from Burma," 6 February 1946.

[119] GA CSO 4-67, OC Troops Gambia to Colonial Secretary, Bathurst, 8 May 1946.

[120] Haywood and Clarke, *The History of the Royal West African Frontier Force*, 474.

[121] John Siblon, "Negotiating Hierarchy and Memory: African and Caribbean Troops from Former British Coloniesin London's Imperial Spaces," *The London Journal* 41, no. 3 (September 1, 2016): 299–312. See also James K. Matthews, "World War I and the Rise of African Nationalism: Nigerian Veterans as Catalysts of Change," *The Journal of Modern African Studies* 20, no. 3 (1982): 493–502.

Conclusion

[1] NA CO 445-55, Governor Armitage to the Colonial Secretary, 11 February 1921.

[2] Haywood and Clarke, *The History of the Royal West African Frontier Force*, 478.

[3] NA CO 968-610, Governor Wyn-Harris to Secretary of State for the Colonies, 14 January 1958. ORDP, Memoirs of Major G.G. Allt.

[4] David Perfect, *Historical Dictionary of The Gambia*, Fifth Edition (Lanham: Rowman & Littlefield, 2016), 168.

[5] Hughes and Perfect, *A Political History of The Gambia, 1816-1994*, 152-153.

[6] Maggie Dwyer, "Fragmented Forces: The Development of the Gambian Military," *African Security Review* 26, no.4 (October 2, 2017): 362–77.

[7] Ibid., 365. For the military history of the Gambia after independence also consult Hughes and Perfect, *A Political History of The Gambia, 1816-1994* and Dwyer, *Soldiers in Revolt*.

Bibliography

Archives and Other Primary Sources
African Mail
National Archives of the United Kingdom
RWAFF News
The Gambia National Archives
The London Gazette
The Oxford Records Development Project at Weston Library, Oxford

Published Works

Anderson, Benedict. *Imagined Communities: Reflections on the Origin and Spread of Nationalism.* London: Verso, 2016.

Anderson, Richard. "The Diaspora of Sierra Leone's Liberated Africans: Enlistment, Forced Migration, and 'Liberation' at Freetown, 1808-1863." *African Economic History* 41, no.1 (2013): 101–38.

Anderson, Ross. *The Battle of Tanga 1914.* Charleston: Tempus Publishing Inc., 2002.

———. *The Forgotten Front: The East African Campaign, 1914 -1918.* The History Press, 2014.

Balesi, Charles John. *From Adversaries to Comrades-in-Arms: West Africans and the French Military, 1885-1918.* Waltham, Mass.: Crossroads Press, 1979.

Black, Jeremy. *The Atlantic Slave Trade in World History.* London: Routledge, 2015.

Buckley, Roger N. *The British Army in the West Indies: Society and the Military in the Revolutionary Age.* Gainesville: University Press of Florida, 1998.

———. "The British Army's African Recruitment Policy, 1790-1807." *A Journal of African and Afro-American Studies* 5, no. 2 (2008): 1–12.

Bush, Barbara. *Imperialism, Race, and Resistance: Africa and Britain, 1919-1945.* London:Routledge, 1999.

Byfield, Judith, Carolyn Brown, Timothy Parsons, and Ahmad Alawad Sikainga, eds. *Africa andWorld War II.* New York: Cambridge University Press, 2015.

Byfield, Judith. "Producing for the War." In *Africa and World War II*, edited by Judith Byfield, Carolyn Brown, Timothy Parsons, and Ahmad Alawad Sikainga. New York: CambridgeUniversity Press, 2015.

Chamberlain, Muriel Evelyn. *The Scramble for Africa.* New York: Routledge, 2013.

Clayton, Anthony, and David Killingray. *Khaki and Blue: Military and Police in British*

Colonial Africa. Athens, Ohio: Ohio University Center for International Studies, 1989.

Cole, Festus. "Defining the 'Flesh' of the Black Soldier in Colonial Sierra Leone: Background to the Gunners' Mutiny of 1939." *Canadian Journal of African Studies / Revue Canadienne Des Études Africaines* 48, no. 2 (May 4, 2014): 275–95.

———. "Sierra Leone and World War 1." PhD Dissertation, University of London - School of Oriental and African Studies, 1994.

Denzer, LaRay. "Wallace-Johnson and the Sierra Leone Labor Crisis of 1939." *African StudiesReview* 25, no. 2/3 (1982): 159–83.

Downes, W. D. *With the Nigerians in East Africa.* London: Methuen & Co, 1919.

Dwyer, Maggie. "Fragmented Forces: The Development of the Gambian Military." *African Security Review* 26, no. 4 (October 2, 2017): 362–77.

———. *Soldiers in Revolt: Army Mutinies in Africa.* Oxford: Oxford University Press, 2017.

Dyde, Brian. *The Empty Sleeve: The Story of the West India Regiments of the British Army.* London: Hansib, 1997.

Echenberg, Myron. *Colonial Conscripts: The Tirailleurs Sénégalais in French West Africa, 1857-1960.* Portsmouth, NH: Heinemann, 1991.

Ekoko, Edho. "The Strategic-Imperial Factor in British Expansion in Sierra Leone, 1882-1899." *Journal of the Historical Society of Nigeria* 11, no. 1/2 (1981): 138–52.

———. "The West African Frontier Force Revisited." *Journal of the Historical Society of Nigeria* 10, no. 1 (1979): 47–63.

Farwell, Byron. *The Great War in Africa.* New York: W.W. Norton & Company, 1986.

Fox-Godden, Aimée. "Beyond the Western Front: The Practice of Inter-Theatre Learning in the British Army during the First World War." *War in History*

23, no. 2 (2016): 190–209.

French, David. *Military Identities: The Regimental System, the British Army, and the British People, c.1870-2000*. Oxford: Oxford University Press, 2005.

———. *Raising Churchill's Army: The British Army and the War Against Germany 1919-1945*. Oxford: Oxford University Press, 2000.

Gailey, Harry A. *A History of the Gambia*. London: Routledge & Kegan Paul, 1964.

Ginio, Ruth. *French Colonialism Unmasked: The Vichy Years in French West Africa*. Lincoln: University of Nebraska Press, 2006.

Gorges, E. Howard. *The Great War in West Africa*. East Sussex: The Naval & Military Press, 1916.

Gray, J.M. *A History of the Gambia*. London: Frank Cass & Co, 1940.

Hamilton, John. *War Bush: 81 (West African) Division in Burma 1943-1945*. Norwich: Michael Russell Publishing Ltd, 2001.

Handloff, Robert E. "Prayers, Amulets, and Charms: Health and Social Control." *African Studies Review* 25, no. 2/3 (1982): 185–94.

Harrison, Mark. "Medicine and the Culture of Command: The Case of Malaria Control in the British Army during the Two World Wars." *Medical History* 40, no. 4 (1996): 437–452.

———. *Medicine and Victory: British Military Medicine in the Second World War*. Oxford: Oxford University Press, 2004.

———. "The British Army and the Problem of Venereal Disease in France and Egypt during the First World War." *Medical History* 39, no. 2 (1995): 133–158.

Hatton, P. H. S. "The Gambia, the Colonial Office, and the Opening Months of the First World War." *The Journal of African History* 7, no. 1 (1966): 123–31.

Haywood, A., and F. A. S. Clarke. *The History of the Royal West African Frontier Force*. Aldershot: Gale & Polden Ltd, 1964.

Hodges, Geoffrey. *The Carrier Corps: Military Labor in the East African Campaign, 1914-1918*. New York: Greenwood Press, 1986.

Hordern, Charles. *Military Operations: East Africa*. London: H.M. Stationery Office, 1941.

Hughes, Arnold, and David Perfect. *A Political History of The Gambia, 1816-1994*. Rochester: University of Rochester Press, 2006.

———. "Trade Unionism in the Gambia." *African Affairs* 88, no. 353 (1989): 549–72.

Ibhawoh, Bonny. "Second World War Propoganda, Imperial Idealism and Anti-

Colonial
Nationalism in British West Africa." *Nordic Journal of African Studies* 16, no. 2 (2007):221–43.

Igbino, John. *Spidermen: Nigerian Chindits and Wingate's Operation Thursday Burma 1943-1944*. Bloomington, IN: Author House, 2018.

Jackson, Ashley. *The British Empire and the Second World War*. London: Hambledon Continuum, 2006.

Jennings, Eric T. *Free French Africa in World War II: The African Resistance*. New York: Cambridge University Press, 2015.

Jesman, Czeslaw. "The Polish Experiment in West Africa During World War II." *Instituto Italiano per l'Africa e l'Oriente* 20, no. 4 (1965): 413–26.

Johnson, Marion. "The Slaves of Salaga." *The Journal of African History* 27, no. 2 (1986): 341–62.

Jones, Spencer. *From Boer War to World War: Tactical Reform of the British Army, 1902-1914*. Norman: University of Oklahoma Press, 2012.

Killingray, David, and James Matthews. "Beasts of Burden: British West African Carriers in the First World War." *Canadian Journal of African Studies / Revue Canadienne Des Études Africaines* 13, no. 1/2 (1979): 5–23.

Killingray, David, and Richard Rathbone, eds. *Africa and the Second World War*. New York: Palgrave Macmillan, 1986.

Killingray, David. *Fighting for Britain: African Soldiers in the Second World War*. Woodbridge: Boydell & Brewer Ltd, 2010.

———. "Labour Exploitation for Military Campaigns in British Colonial Africa 1870-1945." *Journal of Contemporary History* 24, no. 3 (1989): 483–501.

———. "Labour Mobilisation in British Colonial Africa for the War Effort, 1939-46." In *Africa and the Second World War*, 68–96. New York: Palgrave Macmillan, 1986.

———. "The Idea of a British Imperial African Army." *The Journal of African History* 20, no. 3 (1979): 421–36.

———. "The Mutiny of the West African Regiment in the Gold Coast, 1901." *The International Journal of African Historical Studies* 16, no. 3 (1983): 441–54.

———. "The 'Rod of Empire': The Debate over Corporal Punishment in the British African Colonial Forces, 1888-1946." *The Journal of African History* 35, no. 2 (1994): 201–16.

Law, Robin, ed. *From Slave Trade to "Legitimate" Commerce: The Commercial Transition in Nineteenth-Century West Africa*. Cambridge: Cambridge University Press, 1995.

Lawler, Nancy Ellen. *Soldiers, Airmen, Spies, and Whisperers: The Gold Coast in World War II*. Athens, Ohio: Ohio University Press, 2002.

Lee, R. Alton. "The Army 'Mutiny' of 1946." *The Journal of American History* 53, no. 3 (1966):555–71.

Lettow-Vorbeck, Paul Emil von. *My Reminiscences of East Africa*. Ravenio Books, 1920.

Lovejoy, Paul E. *Jihād in West Africa during the Age of Revolutions*. Athens, Ohio: Ohio University Press, 2016.

———. *Transformations in Slavery: A History of Slavery in Africa*. 3rd ed. Cambridge: Cambridge University Press, 2011.

Lunn, Joe. "'Les Races Guerrierès': Racial Preconceptions in the French Military about West African Soldiers during the First World War." *Journal of Contemporary History* 34, no. 4 (1999): 517–36.

———. *Memoirs of the Maelstrom: A Senegalese Oral History of the First World War*. Portsmouth, NH: Heinemann, 1999.

Maddox, Gregory. "Mtunya: Famine in Central Tanzania, 1917-20." *The Journal of African History* 31, no. 2 (1990): 181–97.

Mann, Gregory. *Native Sons: West African Veterans and France in the Twentieth Century*. Durham: Duke University Press, 2006.

Matthews, James K. "World War I and the Rise of African Nationalism: Nigerian Veterans as Catalysts of Change." *The Journal of Modern African Studies* 20, no. 3 (1982): 493–502.

McLynn, Frank. *The Burma Campaign: Disaster into Triumph 1942-45*. New Haven: Yale University Press, 2010.

Miners, N. J. *The Nigerian Army 1956-1966*. London: Methuen, 1971.

Moberly, F. J. *Military Operations, Togoland and the Cameroons, 1914-1916*. London: Imperial War Museum, Dept. of Printed Books, 1931.

Mohamed, Jama. "The 1937 Somaliland Camel Corps Mutiny: A Contrapuntal Reading." *The International Journal of African Historical Studies* 33, no. 3 (2000): 615–34.

Mordi, Emmanuel Nwafor. "'No Longer Required for Operations': Troops' Repatriation to West Africa after the Second World War, 1945–1950." *The Journal of Imperial and Commonwealth History*, June 9, 2020, 1–30.

Moyd, Michelle. "Centring a Sideshow: Local Experiences of the First World War in Africa." *First World War Studies* 7, no. 2 (May 3, 2016): 111–30.

———. *Violent Intermediaries: African Soldiers, Conquest, and Everyday Colonialism in German East Africa*. Athens, Ohio: Ohio University Press, 2014.

Moyse-Bartlett, H. *The King's African Rifles: A Study in the Military History of*

East andCentral Africa, 1890-1945. England: Naval & Military Press, 1956.

Njung, George. "Soldiers of Their Own: Honor, Violence, Resistance and Conscription in Colonial Cameroon during the First World War." PhD Dissertation, University of Michigan, 2016.

O'Brien, Phillips. *How the War Was Won: Air-Sea Power and Allied Victory in World War II.* Cambridge: Cambridge University Press, 2015.

Omissi, David E. *Air Power and Colonial Control: The Royal Air Force 1919-1939*. Manchester: Manchester University Press, 1990.

Osborne, Myles. *Ethnicity and Empire in Kenya: Loyalty and Martial Race among the Kamba, c.1800 to the Present.* New York, NY: Cambridge University Press, 2014.

Owusu-Ansah, David. "Islamic Influence in a Forest Kingdom: The Role of Protective Amuletsin Early 19th Century Asante." *Transafrican Journal of History* 12 (1983): 100–133.

———. "Prayer, Amulets, and Healing." In *The History of Islam in Africa*, edited by N Levtzion and R Pouwels. Athens: Ohio University Press, 2000.

Page, Melvin, ed. *Africa and the First World War*. New York: Palgrave Macmillan, 1987.

Paice, Edward. *Tip and Run: The Untold Tragedy of the Great War in Africa.* London: Weidenfeld & Nicolson, 2007.

Parsons, Timothy. *The African Rank-and-File: Social Implications of Colonial Military Servicein the King's African Rifles, 1902-1964.* Portsmouth, NH: Heinemann, 1999.

Pearson, Michael. *The Burma Air Campaign, 1941-1945*. South Yorkshire: Pen & Sword Books Ltd., 2006.

Perfect, David. *Historical Dictionary of The Gambia*. Fifth Edition. Lanham: Rowman & Littlefield, 2016.

Peterson, Derek R., ed. *Abolitionism and Imperialism in Britain, Africa, and the Atlantic*. Athens, Ohio: Ohio University Press, 2010.

Phillips, Barnaby. *Another Man's War: The Story of a Burma Boy in Britain's Forgotten African Army*. London: Oneworld Publications, 2014.

Pratt, William. "Medicine and Obedience: Canadian Army Morale, Discipline and Surveillance in the Second World War, 1939-1945." PhD Dissertation, University of Calgary, 2015.

Raugh, Harold E. *The Victorians at War, 1815-1914: An Encyclopedia of British Military History*. Santa Barbara: ABC-CLIO, 2004.

Rees, Siân. *Sweet Water and Bitter: The Ships That Stopped the Slave Trade.* Durham, NH: University of New Hampshire Press, 2011.

Scanlan, Padraic X. *Freedom's Debtors: British Antislavery in Sierra Leone in the Age of Revolution*. New Haven: Yale University Press, 2017.
Siblon, John. "Negotiating Hierarchy and Memory: African and Caribbean Troops from Former British Colonies in London's Imperial Spaces." *The London Journal* 41, no. 3 (September 1, 2016): 299–312.
Skinner, David E. "Islam in Kombo: The Spiritual and Militant Jihād of Fodé Ibrahim Silla Turé." *Islamic Africa* 3, no. 1 (2012): 87–126.
Slim, William. *Defeat into Victory*. London: Cassell & Co Ltd., 1956.
Stapleton, Timothy. "Barracks Islam and Command Christianity: Religion in Britain's West African Colonial Army (c.1900–1960)." *War & Society* 39, no. 1 (January 2, 2020): 1–22.
———. "Martial Identities in Colonial Nigeria (c.1900-1960)." *Journal of African Military History* 3, no. 1 (2019): 1–32.
———. *No Insignificant Part: The Rhodesia Native Regiment and the East Africa Campaign of the First World War*. Waterloo, Ont.: Wilfrid Laurier University Press, 2006.
———. "The Africanization of British Imperial Forces in the East African Campaign." In *Turning Point 1917: The British Empire at War*, edited by Douglas Delaney and Nikolas Gardner. Vancouver: UBC Press, 2017.
———. *West African Soldiers in Britain's Colonial Army, 1860-1960*. Rochester, N.Y.: University of Rochester Press, 2022.
Stewart, Andrew. "An Enduring Commitment: The British Military's Role in Sierra Leone." *Defence Studies* 8, no. 3 (September 1, 2008): 351–68.
———. *The First Victory: The Second World War and the East Africa Campaign*. New Haven:Yale University Press, 2016.
Strachan, Hew. *The First World War in Africa*. Oxford: Oxford University Press, 2004.
Streets, Heather. *Martial Races: The Military, Race and Masculinity in British Imperial Culture, 1857-1914*. Manchester: Manchester University Press, 2004.
Thomas, Martin. *Violence and Colonial Order: Police, Workers and Protest in the European Colonial Empires, 1918-1940*. Cambridge: Cambridge University Press, 2012.
Ukpabi, S. C. "The Origins of the West African Frontier Force." *Journal of the Historical Society of Nigeria* 3, no. 3 (1966): 485–501.
———. "West Indian Troops and the Defense of British West Africa in the Nineteenth Century." *African Studies Review* 17, no. 1 (1974): 133–50.
Westwood, Sarah Davis. "Ceddo, Sòfa, Tirailleur: Slave Status and Military Identity in Nineteenth-Century Senegambia." *Slavery & Abolition* 39, no.

3 (July 3, 2018): 518–39.

Williams, John. *The Guns of Dakar: September 1940*. London: Heinemann, 1976.

PRAXIS TACTICUM

THE ART, SCIENCE AND PRACTICE OF MILITARY TACTICS

COLONEL CHARLES S. OLIVIERO

PRAXIS TACTICUM
The Art, Science and Practice of Military Tactics

"Praxis Tacticum" will help young leaders learn and master modern combat team tactics...It's a fascinating series of intellectual and practical exercises which will help those leading fast moving and hard-hitting troops in combat, a unique blend of both the science and art of war.
Lieutenant-General (ret'd) The Hon. Andrew Leslie, PC, CMM, MSC, MSM, CD, MA, PhD

Chuck brings the discussion on tactics to the 'centre of gravity' between operational and theoretical perspectives. Praxis Tacticum is for professionals, people interested in tactics and the general reader of history.
Major-General (ret'd) David Fraser, CMM, MSC, MSM, CD

Pundits the world over have long predicted the end of conventional warfare but for the foreseeable future, it is here to stay. Counter insurgency, guerrilla warfare, terrorism, peace enforcement, policing duties. All of these forms, like conventional warfare, are as old as mankind. Modern militaries claim that they are professional bodies, responsible to teach, control and discipline their members. But at least one aspect of this claim is poorly executed: tactics are not taught to junior leaders, which is why this practical guide is essential reading for all junior leaders, officers and NCOs alike.

There is an old military adage that there is no teacher like the enemy. True; but the wise commander will prepare to meet that enemy and become the teacher and not the student.

About the Author

Colonel Chuck Oliviero spent four decades in the Canadian Armed Forces as an Armoured Cavalry officer. He spent half of his career either as a student or as a teacher and the other half commanding troops.

ABOUT THE AUTHOR

Charles Estep is an Active-Duty Air Force Officer currently undergoing rotary wing pilot training at Ft. Rucker, Alabama. He is a 2019 graduate of the United States Air Force Academy with a B.S. in History and Political Science. In 2020, Charles earned his Master's in History from the University of Calgary with a focus on West African Military History.